TRAIN YOUR BRAIN TO
GET HAPPY

TRAIN YOUR BRAIN TO
GET HAPPY

THE SIMPLE PROGRAM THAT PRIMES YOUR GRAY CELLS FOR
JOY, OPTIMISM, AND SERENITY

Teresa Aubele, PhD, Stan Wenck, EdD, and Susan Reynolds

Avon, Massachusetts

Published by
Adams Media, a division of F+W Media, Inc.
57 Littlefield Street, Avon, MA 02322. U.S.A.
www.adamsmedia.com

Contains material adapted and abridged from *The Everything® Family Nutrition Book* by Leslie Bil-
derback, Technical Review by Sandra K. Nissenberg, MS, RD, copyright © 2009 by F+W Media,
Inc., ISBN 10: 1-59869-704-8, ISBN 13: 978-1-59869-704-9; *The Everything® Superfoods Book*
by Delia Quigley, C.N.C., with Brierley E. Wright, RD, copyright © 2008 by F+W Media, Inc.,
ISBN 10: 1-59869-682-3, ISBN 13: 978-1-59869-682-0; and *365 Ways to Boost Your Brain Power*
by Carolyn Dean, MD, Valentine Dmitriev, PhD, and Donna Raskin, copyright © 2009 by F+W
Media Inc., ISBN 10: 1-60550-060-7, ISBN 13: 978-1-60550-060-7.

ISBN 10: 1-4405-1181-0
ISBN 13: 978-1-4405-1181-3
eISBN 10: 1-4405-2668-0
eISBN 13: 978-1-4405-2668-8

Printed in the United States of America.

10 9 8 7 6 5 4 3 2 1

Library of Congress Cataloging-in-Publication Data
is available from the publisher.

This book is available at quantity discounts for bulk purchases.
For information, please call 1-800-289-0963.

DEDICATION

"It is not the brains that matter most, but that which guides them."
—Fyodor Dostoyevsky

For my mother, Nona, my father, Fred, and my sister, Cindy: whose guidance, love, and unwavering faith led me to where I am. Thank you.

—Terri

To Brooke and Brett Aved, who challenged my brain in a multitude of ways and whose very existence has brought me more happiness than words can ever express.

—Susan

CONTENTS

INTRODUCTION

You just want to be happy, right? Of course; it's what everyone wants. Yet only some of us manage to live a happy life—and it's not who you might think it is. It's not the rich or the beautiful or the smart or even those lucky people who were seemingly born happy.

The happiest people are those who have trained their brains to make them happy. And that's something we can all do—no matter what our age or IQ or income or circumstance. In this book, we'll show you how you can harness the power of your brain to get happy—and lead the joyful, adventurous, fulfilled life you've always dreamed of.

The study of the brain—neuroscience—has been evolving for many years, and the amount of new information and discoveries about the brain has been rapidly increasing since the inception of the field. Many studies had been focused on detailing the complex anatomy of the brain, tracing its inputs and outputs via nerves and neurons, understanding learning and memory, and studying how things go awry in injury and mental illness. Then, in the last couple of decades, a game-changing idea emerged from research done by several prominent members of the neuroscience community: The brain is not a rigid organ that remains unchanged throughout the course of your life, like your heart or liver or lungs. Your brain is moldable, bendable—"plastic"—and the situations that you experience throughout your life sculpt your brain into a unique structure built for *you*, the individual. Studies based on this idea have caused an explosion of neuroscience: In total, more neuroscientific research studies have been performed in the past decade than in the prior fifty years *combined*.

Many researchers are now starting to realize the value of studying how to make things go right in your brain—giving birth to the science of happy, joyful, well-functioning brains and how to make and keep them this way, called *affective neuroscience*. This field is all about improving and expanding your brain functioning to quiet or counteract emotional and behavioral problems, using your mind to improve your brain, and giving any individual the tools to create a more fulfilling, happy life.

This book is meant to explain and summarize some of these ground-breaking studies in the field of neuroscience, and to help you use the amazing ideas within them, so you can change the way you think about your brain, your mind, and your life. It will show you how to use studies and ideas developed by neuroscientists, doctors, and psychologists in order to help you achieve the goals of happiness, joyfulness, and peace by *taking control* of your own brain and making it work for you.

So come on, what are you waiting for? Get happy!

—Teresa M. Aubele, PhD, Neuroscience

CHAPTER 1

HAPPINESS IS ALL IN YOUR BRAIN

"From the brain and the brain alone arise our pleasures, joys, laughter and jests, as well as our sorrows, pains and griefs."

—Hippocrates

Getting happy is not rocket science—it's brain science. Brain science tells us that there are many factors that can contribute to your overall sense of happiness. Before we get going, let's take stock of where you stand now.

The Happy Brain Quiz

1. **Each night, you sleep an average of:**
   A. Seven and a half hours or more
   B. Six to seven hours
   C. Four to six hours
   D. Sleep? Who needs sleep?

2. **When you're stressed out, you:**
   A. Go to yoga class
   B. Walk on the treadmill
   C. Have a martini
   D. Pick a fight with your spouse

3. **Your idea of a good meal is:**
   A. Red beans and brown rice
   B. Sushi
   C. Big Mac
   D. Martini

1

4. You weigh:
   A. What you weighed in high school
   B. Fifteen pounds more than you should
   C. Thirty pounds more than you should
   D. Fifty or more pounds more than you should

5. You think of yourself as:
   A. An athlete
   B. More physically active than most
   C. Not as physically active as you should be
   D. A couch potato and proud of it

6. You fall in love:
   A. Again with your spouse every day
   B. As often as you can
   C. Only when you can't avoid it
   D. Under no circumstances—love stinks

7. You're having sex:
   A. As often as possible
   B. Three times a week
   C. Once a month if you're lucky
   D. Never—sex is overrated

8. Your idea of a good brain challenge is:
   A. Learning a new language
   B. Playing a game of chess
   C. Doing a crossword puzzle
   D. Watching *Wheel of Fortune*

9. You describe yourself as:
   A. An optimist
   B. A realist
   C. A pessimist
   D. A fatalist

10. Your idea of fun is:
   A. Something new and adventurous
   B. Being out in nature
   C. Going to the movies
   D. Fun is for kids

Now tally up your score.

- *If you checked mostly As,* you are relatively happy, but with a better understanding of your brain, you can boost your happiness quotient substantially.
- *If you checked mostly Bs,* you do experience happiness but not as often nor as deeply as you could if you were to train your brain to maximize every opportunity for pleasure.
- *If you checked mostly Cs,* you are happiness deprived. You need to nurture your brain, which in turn will nurture your physical and emotional well-being.
- *If you checked mostly Ds,* you are not experiencing the happiness that is every person's birthright. But train your brain, and you can transform your life—and be all the happier for it.

HAPPINESS BEFORE MODERN BRAIN SCIENCE

Hippocrates had it right—way back in the fifth century B.C. Unfortunately, it has taken science more than 2,500 years to officially validate Hippocrates's hypothesis: Our brains *are* the source of our emotions.

In a prescientific era, however, human beings created mythologies such as tales of gods, spirits, witches, and other external supernatural creatures to explain the genesis of feelings, such as love, anger, and happiness. By literally touching the organs of newly deceased people, Aristotle (384–322 B.C.), observed that their brains felt "very cool" while their hearts were still warm. He also touched the brains of live animals and found that the animals did not react at all to the stimulation. (He had no way of knowing that the brain has no touch/pain receptors on its surface.) Aristotle also noticed that the size of the blood vessels around the human brain were very small in comparison to those near the heart, and thus believed that the heart needed more blood to perform something more complex and that the brain, having very little "hot" blood, served to cool the body and regulate temperature.

He thereby concluded:

- That the brain's major function was to cool the head so animals and humans did not overheat.
- That the heart continued to perform more complex functions up until the point of death.
- That the "hot and fiery" blood in the heart contained our "hot and fiery" characters or souls.

Even though Aristotle later expanded his views, for centuries, many humans believed that love and happiness blossomed or withered within our heart chambers, dragging our poor brains along for the ride.

In the late nineteenth century, psychiatrists such as Sigmund Freud, Carl Jung, and William James dedicated their professional lives to studying emotions and behavior. Yet they stood pretty much alone in the scientific community in their beliefs that emotions and behavior could be linked to the physiological workings of the human brain. Unfortunately, there simply wasn't any scientific evidence to support their findings, or to prove or disprove their theories.

What Is Happiness?

What is happiness to you? Happiness is purely subjective and intensely personal. What floats your boat may not be what floats someone else's. Fundamentally, most humans require certain basic, primal, biological needs to be fulfilled—hunger, thirst, shelter, love, sex, etc.—before a discussion about happiness can commence. Beyond that, the closest we can come to a general definition of happiness is that it is a pervasive and long-lasting sensation of well-being.

Many of Freud's theories, in particular, were based solely on behavioral observation. Some were even rooted in faulty observation, wherein he skewed results to prove his hypothesis that emotional problems were rooted in suppressed memories. Despite these questions about his research methods, Freud's ideas remain pervasive in our culture.

Thanks to modern brain-scanning machinery such as magnetic resonance imagery (MRI) and functional magnetic resonance imagery (fMRI), neuroscientists now have reliable methods to more fully investigate and study physiological connections to human behavior, and they have begun testing old theories and formulating new theories based on behavioral *and* biological evidence.

What Are MRI and fMRI?

MRI is a technique used in radiology to readily show soft tissues of the body, like the brain, by using a powerful magnetic field to scan whatever area of the body is being studied. An fMRI (functional MRI) measures the change in blood flow related to brain activity in real time. We'll be using these terms throughout the book, as they've both proven very helpful in discovering which areas of the brain respond to what activities and in tracking changes in the brain.

AND THEN CAME DRUGS

Recent strides in the field of psychopharmacology have also helped clarify brain activity. Consider the following findings:

- While studying antihistamines, researchers discovered that certain medications had a positive effect on psychosis, which led to antipsychotic drugs.
- When researching drugs designed to treat tuberculosis, doctors discovered that certain drugs elevated subjects' moods, which led to antidepressants.
- An Australian doctor discovered that lithium made guinea pigs docile, which led to drugs that help manage the mania side of manic-depressive disorder, better known now as bipolar disorder. (Scientists

still have no idea what lithium actually does to help bipolar patients. It remains a neuroscientific mystery.)

As these discoveries mounted, it became harder to cling to Freudian concepts—for example, that neuroses and psychoses were caused solely by childhood traumas, or that repression or intentional suppression of sexual desires fully explained human emotional frailty. Instead, researchers embrace the theory that aberrant brain chemistry likely plays a major role in mental and emotional dysfunction. No one disputes that environment plays a huge role, as well, but the fact that depression, obsessive-compulsive disorder (OCD), and bipolar disorder respond remarkably well to drug therapy has led to major breakthroughs in the study of brain physiology as it relates to emotional dysfunction.

THE ADVENT OF HAPPINESS AS A SCIENCE

Seeking happiness as a life goal is a relatively new idea. Back in the days when people had to work night and day merely to provide for themselves and their families, there wasn't time for the pursuit of happiness. Granted, it was always the ideal—and was clearly identified as one of our most basic rights in our Constitution. In reality, however, only the very wealthy had the luxury of time to worry about whether or not they were happy.

Then, two things occurred that changed everything:

1. Thanks to modernization and a healthy economy, during the 1960s, more people began to have spare time and energy (not spent on fulfilling basic needs) to ponder what they wanted out of life and to pursue what would make them happier.
2. The wildly successful introduction of Prozac in 1988 made millions of people feel artificially happy—and concurrently realize that they still weren't *really* happy with their lives.

No Time for Happiness

Few people in the WWI and WWII generations talked about living a *fulfilled* life. Living was about duty and responsibility to family and country. A man was expected to marry, and a married man had to work hard in order to provide for his family. Most lower- and middle-class men could do little more than collapse when they got home, too tired to pursue much of anything enjoyable. Women, of course, were busy taking care of the home, raising their children, and tending to their husbands. Post-WWII, when women joined the work force in droves, their "liberated" lives only became *more* complicated and demanding, not less.

What Do Millionaires and Slum Dwellers Have in Common?

One study found that American multimillionaires rated their happiness levels (on average) around 5.8 on a scale of 1 to 7. That seems fairly high, but when you compare it to slum dwellers in Calcutta who rated their happiness at 4.6 (who were one step above being homeless; homeless people rated their happiness at 2.9), you begin to see that having money is relevant only to a point. Psychologists call this the "paradox of happy peasants and miserable millionaires" and note that these findings indicate that money has a correlative, but not a causative, effect when it comes to happiness. In other words, happiness is related to money but money alone doesn't provide happiness.

Prozac Nation

In the 1950s antidepressants existed, but family doctors were afraid to prescribe them. They were so potent that it didn't take many for suicidal people to, purposefully or accidentally, off themselves. Even one week's portion of the pills could prove fatal.

Thus, when Prozac was introduced to the world, its biggest attraction was that it wouldn't kill anyone, even if that person intentionally consumed an overdose. Plus, Prozac came with surprising benefits: It could provide relief from symptoms of a long list of lesser maladies, such as anxiety, hostility, fearfulness, low self-confidence, PMS, and even heartache. Naturally the masses became enchanted, so much so that the word *serotonin* entered our national vocabulary and a book entitled *Prozac Nation* became a bestseller. However, even with their moods stabilized, many people began to notice that they still weren't *truly* happy.

Guru Nation

At that point, the baby boomers arrived—worldwide, not solely in America. In observing their parents' lives, these "rich by comparison," pampered youth decided that mind expansion and emotional fulfillment were well worth pursuing. Prior to (and post) Prozac, some popped pills, smoked marijuana, tried psychotropic drugs like LSD, and ingested mind-altering substances such as peyote and mushrooms to expand their minds.

The Difference Between Neuroscience and Psychobiology

Neuroscience is the scientific study of the nervous system, including the brain. *Psychobiology* (a.k.a Physiological Psychology) is the application of biological principles (in particular the principles of neuroscience) to the study of mental processes and behavior in human and nonhuman animals.

By the time the 1980s rolled around and the baby boomers realized that their lives were no simpler, no happier, and that they had essentially sold out and gone down the same path as their parents, they went in search of happiness gurus and therapists and created a whole new, highly lucrative book genre: self-help.

Only then, when throngs of dissatisfied baby boomers began to squawk, did scientists in the field of psychology begin to study happiness with any real vigor. To wit, in the last twenty or so years, more than 3,000 scientific articles on happiness have been published. We got obsessed and stayed obsessed with happiness, so much so there's a popular online database (Worlddatabaseofhappiness.eur.nl) that collects and analyzes happiness studies from all over the world. (By the way, the United States ranked twentieth on the happiness scale in 2010, scoring a 7.4 on a 10-point scale, but more on that later.) There is also an official *Journal of Happiness Studies*, a peer-reviewed scientific journal devoted to reporting on the pursuit of subjective well-being through science.

What Science Can't Cover

Even as we learn more and more about the human brain and how all those marvelous and ingenious neurons and neurotransmitters function, the gathering of empirical evidence will always have to be balanced with the heart—the human mind and soul, and the role they play in our pursuit of happiness. Not all of our unwieldy emotions can, or should, be treated with drugs. Neuroscience and psychobiology will always have to factor in the role environmental or situational sadness or joy or rage plays. Without question, we are a mixture of genetic, biological, chemical, and emotional beings. But first, let's talk about the origins of mind science.

THE ORIGINS OF MIND SCIENCE

"If you are distressed by anything external (or internal), the pain is not due to the thing itself, but to your estimate of it . . . and this you have the power to revoke at any moment."

—Marcus Aurelius, describing emotional regulation, approximately 2,100 years ago

Traditionally, human nature, along with the nature of the mind, had been thought of as not only completely inherited but often divinely ordained. Individuals, or groups of people, were considered to be, by nature, superior or inferior either because of their parentage or because of the will of a higher power. In contrast to this doctrine was the idea of the *tabula rasa*: the blank slate. This idea seemed to have first appeared in the writings of Aristotle, who spoke of the mind as an "unscribed tablet" in what is considered the first Western textbook of psychology: *De Anima* (*On the Soul*).

Does Money Make Us Happy?

It depends. Though you may immediately assume that money would be one of the most likely sources of happiness, it's not always the case. Multiple studies have found that having money beyond a certain level (around $50,000 to $75,000 in annual income) in America doesn't vastly improve happiness levels. If someone is living at or below the poverty level, having enough annual income to move up the economic scale (even if only as far as the middle class) will make them happier, but mostly because it allows them to fulfill their basic needs, such as shelter and food, more easily.

In the eleventh century, the theory of *tabula rasa* was developed more clearly by the Islamic philosopher Avicenna, who argued that the "human intellect at birth is rather like a *tabula rasa*, a pure potentiality that is actualized through education" and that knowledge is attained through "empirical familiarity with objects in this world from which one abstracts universal concepts." The modern incarnation of this theory is mostly attributed to John Locke's expression of it in *An Essay Concerning Human Understanding* in the seventeenth century. In Locke's philosophy, *tabula rasa* was the theory that the human mind is at birth a "blank slate" without any rules for processing data or storing facts, and that any and all rules for processing are formed solely by one's sensory and life experiences. Locke's theory emphasized the individual's freedom to "author" his or her own soul.

Modern-Day Mind Science

Nowadays, scientists recognize that most of the brain is, in fact, preprogrammed and preorganized in order to process sensory input, motor control, and emotions. In all humans, for example, the occipital lobe at the back of the brain analyzes and processes incoming visual information, and this function does not change from person to person. However, these preprogrammed parts of the brain can learn and refine their ability to perform the tasks for which they are ideally suited.

For example, Steven Pinker, a psychology professor at Harvard University, argues that while the brain is programmed to pick up spoken language easily, it is not programmed to learn to read and write, and a human generally will not spontaneously learn to do so. People can *learn* to read and write, however, by practicing and teaching the parts of our minds that are dedicated to speech to associate written symbols with spoken sounds. Your brain can be trained even at a very young age to do some amazing things!

Thus, it seems that Aristotle, Avicenna, and John Locke had it half right: Your brain at birth is partly a blank slate, but not entirely—different parts of your brain are indeed meant to process specific types of information. However, *how* your brain does this, and *when* and *why* are all things that are entirely up to you. The way that you view the world around you, and the associations that you make, are entirely within *your* ability to shape and control. How exactly this lifelong learning occurs in your brain is one of the most interesting subjects that neuroscience has come to explore.

BREAKTHROUGHS IN BRAIN SCIENCE

Until recently, scientists believed that the human brain and its structures were formed during gestation and infancy and remained pretty much unchanged through childhood. You had a given number of neurons in a specific brain structure, and while the number might vary among people, once you were done with childhood development, you were set in this mold. Your connections were already made, and the learning and growing period of your brain was over. In the last decade, however, researchers have found significant evidence that this is not so, and that something called *neuroplasticity* continues throughout our lives.

What Is Neuroplasticity?

It's important to clarify that neuroscientists use the word "plastic" in a different way than you might be used to. In neuroscience, "plastic" means that a material has the ability to change, to be molded into different shapes. Thus, neuroplasticity is your brain's ability to alter its physical structure, to repair damaged regions, to grow new neurons and get rid of old ones, to rezone regions that performed one task and have them assume a new task, and to change the circuitry that weaves neurons into the networks that allow us to remember, feel, suffer, think, imagine, and dream.

How Neuroplasticity Works in Your Brain

Here's a short list of what scientists now believe your brain is capable of continuing to achieve throughout your life, thanks to neuroplasticity:

1. **It can reactivate long-dormant circuitry.** The expression "it's like riding a bike" is very true when it comes to your brain. Often, you never completely forget a skill once learned, though you might need a short period of practice to kick your neurons back into gear.

2. **It can create new circuitry.** For instance, the neurons in your nose responsible for smell are made new and replaced every few weeks, and new neurons are made in other parts of your brain as well. Also, whenever you learn something new, your brain can strengthen existing neuronal connections and create new synapses that allow you to maximize new skills.

3. **It can rewire circuitry.** Parts of your brain that were used for one purpose can be retasked to other uses. This is often the case with stroke victims who relearn to use a limb or to speak after some neurons are destroyed.

4. **It can quiet aberrant circuits and connections** (such as those leading to depression, posttraumatic stress disorder (PTSD), obsessive-compulsive disorder (OCD), phobias, and so on). Some parts of

your brain can exert control over others and change how much they affect your mood, decision-making, and thought processes.

HOW DOES NEUROPLASTICITY MAKE YOU HAPPIER?

Because of your brain's neuroplasticity, you can train your brain to get happier regardless of your age. Here's why:

1. The actions you take can literally expand or contract different regions of the brain, firing up circuits or tamping them down. Example: If you worry excessively, you are activating certain types of pathways due to habit. You can learn, however, to retrain your brain to quiet these pathways and strengthen others, so it doesn't automatically go down the "worry" highway.

2. The more you ask your brain to do, the more space it sets up to handle the new tasks, often by shrinking or repurposing space that houses your ability to perform rarely used tasks. Example: If you typically go into a melancholy funk when you face problems, your brain will continue that habit. If, however, you instruct your brain to come up with creative solutions to your problems, you can shut down the melancholy pathways by making them less used and smaller, and instead open up and increase use of the creativity workshop in your brain.

3. New brain-scanning technology has shown that conscious perception activates the same brain areas as imagination. In effect, you can neutralize the long-term effects of painful memories by rewriting (or more correctly, rewiring) the past that lives within your brain.

4. Your brain usually cannot reliably distinguish between recorded experience and internal fantasy. If you program your mind with images of you being happy and spend time visualizing the desired images long enough and hard enough, your brain will think those images really happened and will associate happiness with them.

In other words, whatever you ask your brain to do (employing intention, focus, practice, and reinforcement), it will strive to do. It is a tool you can use in whatever way you see fit. The more often you ask your brain to think happy thoughts, the more your brain responds by forging new or beefing up existing neuronal circuitry to light up your happy board, and by weakening the neuronal connections that drain your happy thoughts.

What Would Your fMRI Say about You?

What you do, see, feel, and think is mirrored in the size of your respective brain regions and in the strength of the connections your brain makes. While it's admittedly somewhat spooky, it's already entirely conceivable that a skilled neuroscientist could view an fMRI image of your brain and reasonably ascertain what your talents are; what your thinking, behavioral, or emotional problem areas are; and what you've been up to thus far in your life. Forget about fingerprints and DNA samples; we now have brain images that reveal far more information than we might reasonably want someone else to know—or maybe even more than we want to know.

Congratulations! You are almost ready to train your brain to bury the unproductive, depressing thoughts and habits that drag you (and your brain) down and to shine light on, nourish, and reinforce the productive, cheerful thoughts and activities that recharge your happiness batteries. Here's the beauty in it: By using your thoughts and choosing certain activities, you can lay the groundwork for brain restructuring that will make you happier—and wealthier and sexier, but those are whole other topics. . . .

BREAKTHROUGHS IN THOUGHT PROCESSES

"Strengthening neural systems is not fundamentally different [than strengthening certain muscle groups through physical exercise]. It's basically replacing certain habits of mind with other habits."

—Richard Davidson, PhD

Even more exciting, recent breakthroughs in neuroscience have also shown that your brain can reshape itself and form new synapses *purely from thinking thoughts*. Not only does what you think about and how you think really matter, but *your thoughts can create new realities*. It seems those New Age gurus and their worshipping participants may have been onto something after all. There is now scientific evidence that *if you envision it—thoroughly and often enough—it can come.*

You can think thoughts that reshape your brain, and although outside activities or influences often assist by imprinting and boosting the process, none are *required*. If you think the necessary thoughts—thereby training your brain to act in a new way, strongly *willing* it to do so—and then reinforce this new way of thinking, your brain can change itself, *and the way it works*, to fall in alignment with your thoughts.

The implications for these findings are staggering. It's now not only clear that some emotional and mental illnesses primarily result from errant neurochemistry (some of which can be modified and/or modulated through drug therapies or stimulating new brain connections) but that thoughts *alone* have the ability to alter neuronal connections in a way that can assist in recovery from mental illnesses such as depression, bipolar disorder, phobias, posttraumatic stress disorder (PTSD), and obsessive-compulsive disorder (OCD). Even sociopaths, who are often thought to be hopelessly dysfunctional, may be able to rewire their brains to feel sufficient empathy and compassion to modulate their aberrant, antisocial behavior.

What does all this mean? It means that what you think, do, and say matters—and that it affects who you become on the outside, on the inside, *and* in your brain. Mostly, it means that you can retrain your brain to be more productive, more resilient, and happier.

GROUNDBREAKING STUDIES

We'll mention several groundbreaking studies in the field of neuroscience throughout the book. For now, we'll cover a few of the more important ones and how the results of these studies light the way for helping you train your brain to get happy.

Neuronal Activity/Compassion

Richard Davidson, PhD, a prominent University of Wisconsin psychologist and leader in the relatively new field called affective neuroscience (or contemplative neuroscience due to its focus on the brain science of meditation), has conducted several studies on the effects of a technique known as *mindfulness meditation.* (Mindfulness is a Buddhist practice that we'll discuss in Chapters 4 and 5. Basically, it's a method of learning to focus your mind on being fully present in the here and now.) In one groundbreaking study, Davidson monitored the brain activity of three distinct groups of people: Tibetan Buddhist monks (who had logged 1,500 to 15,000 hours practicing mindfulness meditation, focused on compassion); people who had never meditated; and people who participated in an eight-week meditation training. Davidson and his researchers asked the participants to meditate on compassion and empathy while he monitored their brain activity.

Results

The results of Davidson's study were startling. Among them:

1. When the people who had never meditated were asked to practice a Buddhist compassion meditation, on their first try, meditating stimulated their limbic system (emotional network).
2. When those who had never practiced meditation signed on for eight weeks, as the training progressed, their brains revealed more activity in the left prefrontal cortex (PFC), an area of the brain believed to be responsible for generating positive emotions, such as compassion, empathy, and happiness.

3. When Davidson studied the bran scans of the monks as they meditated, their scans showed significantly higher activity in their left PFCs, so much so the researchers were astounded, describing it as "well out of the normal range."

4. The monks also showed sustained changes in their baseline (i.e., without meditation) brain function, indicating that their meditation practice had changed the way their brains functioned, even when not meditating. These changes were most evident in the left prefrontal cortex.

How This Research Can Help You Get Happy

What Davidson's studies demonstrate is that, even with a relatively small amount of training, fully adult individuals were able to learn a technique that trained them to think differently and to focus on compassion, empathy, and happiness. By training themselves to think differently than they had before, they actually rewired their brains, strengthening pathways associated with happy feelings—after only eight weeks!

The monks, who had had much more practice, showed even more brain differences. The abnormally high activity in the left PFC of the monks suggests that they had formed new neuronal pathways and/or strengthened existing neural connections in this area simply by *thinking*. Meditation as a technique (which we'll cover in depth in Chapter 5) caused their brains to change, not only in response to active thought, but in a fundamental way all the time—even at baseline rest—without thinking about it. Meditation, and thinking about happiness, caused their brains to mold and change, and become wired for more happiness and peace twenty-four hours a day. Talk about the power of positive thinking!

Neurogenesis

Neurogenesis, literally meaning "birth of neurons," is the process by which neurons are formed and the entire brain is populated with them. While this phenomenon is most active before you are born, recent neuroscience has shown that this process continues through puberty, adolescence, and right into adulthood—virtually until you stop learning new skills. The idea of adult neurogenesis was slow to take hold in the neuroscience community—overthrowing a long-held belief (that it was all over in young adulthood) can sometimes be difficult!

Results

Here are various study results pertinent to neurogenesis:

1. The first evidence of adult neurogenesis in mammals was presented by Dr. Joseph Altman in 1962, where he provided solid evidence showing that new neurons formed in the brain of adult rats following brain damage.
2. Dr. Altman followed this initial study with similar demonstrations of adult neurogenesis in a brain area called the hippocampus in 1963.
3. In 1969, Dr. Altman further discovered and named the source of adult-generated neurons in the olfactory bulb, a portion of the brain dedicated to the perception of odors. However, Dr. Altman's careful studies were overwhelmingly ignored by the scientific community at large!
4. In the late 1980s and the 1990s, Dr. Altman's work came back into the spotlight and was replicated and expanded upon by other researchers, such as Dr. Shirley Bayer, Dr. Michael Kaplan, and Dr. Fernando Nottebohm. In studying the brains of mammals and birds, these researchers showed that adult neurogenesis takes place in several brain areas in these animal species, and in the 1990s, human neurogenesis was confirmed.

How This Research Can Help You Get Happy

These landmark studies proved a simple and profound truth: *Your brain can make new neurons*. While most of the early studies showed that new neurons were made in response to brain damage (similar to a stroke), further studies have shown that new neurons are made in many animals in response to experience and training regiments. Furthermore, your neurons can *change*. They are plastic and flexible, and can change the strengths of their connections in a matter of minutes. Yes, in the time it takes you to read this paragraph, your brain can be set on the road to change, to becoming happier and healthier!

Fire Together, Wire Together, Happy Together

Canadian psychologist Dr. Donald Hebb coined a phrase known to neuroscientists the world over: "Neurons that fire together, wire together." This concept describes, in a nutshell, how we learn and how we come to associate things with each other. In other words, it describes how *mental activity changes neural structure*, or how what you think changes your brain! Dr. Hebb developed the theory that it is the timing of neuronal firing that makes for new or changed wiring. Neurons that fire within a few thousandths of a second of each other—basically, neurons that are firing at the same time in response to a thought or experience—can do one of two things: they can strengthen existing synapses or build new synapses.

Results: Hebb's Law

Dr. Hebb combined data from anatomical, behavioral, and psychological analyses of the early twentieth century into a single statement: When neuron A is close to neuron B, and neuron A repeatedly is stimulated enough in order to excite neuron B, some metabolic change occurs that makes neuron A more likely than other neurons to stimulate neuron B. In other words, those two neurons become more linked than the other neurons around them, and that connection takes up more available neural space than it did before.

How This Research Can Help You Get Happy

Dr. Hebb's research has provided fundamental knowledge to neuroscience, and even though Hebb's law was put to paper in 1949, the theory has held up after more than sixty years of research and countless experiments. What this means is that constant associations between neurons make those associations stronger. For example, if you routinely dwell on your resentments, regrets, and other negative emotions, the neurons involved in that particular mental activity will fire busily at the same time and automatically start wiring together as well. This process will add one more bit of neural structure to feeling discontented, angry, or sad.

On the other hand, if you regularly focus on the good feelings around you and inside you, like kindness, compassion, empathy, and patience, then the neurons involved in *those* thoughts will wire together and take up more space, stitching more hopefulness, confidence, and happiness into the fabric of your brain and your self (and taking away space from the negative paths!).

Imagination Is Reality

In an interesting study conducted in 2002, Dr. Nakia Gordon at Bowling Green State University, Ohio, led research that reported that people can feel joy or sorrow simply by imagining those emotions and the types of movement that go along with laughing or crying. Dr. Gordon found that women were able to feel joy and sorrow simply from imagining the physical act of laughing and crying. "Furthermore," she reported, "imagined laughter was effective at reducing sadness, and, imagined crying reduced happiness."

Results

1. In Dr. Gordon's study, twenty women were trained in performing the laughing and crying imagination tasks for three days prior to brain scanning with fMRI. They imagined the physical movements associated with laughter and crying and rated their emotions on a scale of 1 to 9 before and after the imagery.

2. Happy and sad emotions were also induced by using personally meaningful musical selections, which were not thought-generated.

3. Brain activity during both tasks—imagining laughter or crying—showed involvement of brain areas typically associated with the generation of emotions and areas that control movement.

4. Listening to self-selected happy and sad musical selections also produced brain activity associated with emotions and music processing.

How This Research Can Help You Get Happy

The findings of the Bowling Green study revealed that simply *imagining* laughter or crying, without having any external cue, triggered the brain in *the exact same way* as an actual sad or happy event. According to Dr. Gordon, these results "highlight the ability of mental imagery to simulate actual behavior." That means that merely imagining, or focusing on a happy event, can make you *actually* happy in a neurochemical sense and strengthen happiness connections in your brain.

YOUR MARCHING ORDERS

Humans are the only species known to have a conscious awareness that we have brains and bodies capable of adaptability, that we can affect the course our lives take, that we can make choices along the way that vastly affect the quality of our lives—biologically, intellectually, environmentally, and spiritually. As humans, we have the ability to mold our very beings to become what or who we wish to become. While some of us may, indeed, have genetic and biological imperatives that may require medication or training to overcome, or at least to modulate, the vast majority of us do, in fact, hold our emotional destiny in our hands.

Which brings us back to the subject of this book. Can you train your brain for happiness? Yes, dear readers, you can train your brain for happiness. It will require focus, intention, dedication, accountability, action, and persistence, but you can reshape your brain to experience and create greater happiness.

CHAPTER 2

HOW YOUR BRAIN WORKS

"To know the brain . . . is equivalent to ascertaining the material course of thought and will, to discovering the intimate history of life in its perpetual duel with external forces."

—Santiago Ramon y Cajal, neuroanatomist

ONE AMAZING ORGAN

Your brain is, by far, the most complex organ in your body, capable of making tens of thousands of calculations in a second and working faster than any man-made supercomputer. These are some of the highly complex functions your brain provides:

- Monitoring and controlling your breathing, heartbeat, blood circulation, digestion, and all other body functions
- Feeling, interpreting, and responding to pressure, pain, arousal, etc.
- Coordinating all muscle movements
- Experiencing and executing a wide range of moods
- Observing, interpreting, creating, storing, and recalling myriad complex memories
- Connecting memories and thoughts to form complex associations
- Performing abstract thinking
- Creating and integrating your identity
- Regenerating brain cells

And that's the short list! The fact that your brain works so well in performing all of these complicated tasks is nothing less than an amazing triumph of nature. Your brain's most basic, primary function concerning happiness is to receive information from the outside world, process it, compare it to previous information, and make decisions about how to react.

Like any other organ, or even like any more familiar machine, all of your brain parts, from small to large, contribute to keeping your brain in its best possible shape. Understanding how all of those parts ideally work together to create a healthy, happy brain gives you the knowledge to turn your brain into a finely oiled machine that functions at its maximum capacity to create a healthy, happy *you*. Some of the following details may be difficult to grasp when you first read them, but the better you understand them, the better you can direct your energies and personalize how you will train your brain to get happy!

BRAIN ANATOMY 101

The most crucial part of a working brain is also its most basic: the brain cells known as neurons, their billions of helper cells, and how these cells interact with each other. Your brain consists of more than 100 billion cells (10 billion are neurons; 90 billion are "helper" cells) whose primary function is to form synapses for the exchange of electrical and chemical information.

Luckily, your neurons are not bundled into an unorganized mess, communicating information at random. Much like a finely tuned, functional corporation, your brain is organized into different "departments" that specialize in certain types of information—from basic survival information about your body's overall health and present condition to more complex areas that are concerned with thoughts, emotions, and reactions.

Your Brain's Three Sections

In general, there are three major areas of the brain, each containing many structures that work together toward a common goal:

1. **Reptilian.** Your reptilian brain is the most ancient part of your brain, meaning it likely formed the entire brain of early man. It operates behind the scenes and contains all the brain structures that regulate your survival needs: food, oxygen, heart rate, blood pressure, and reproduction, among many others. It's like a silent sentinel that monitors your body and surroundings without your conscious knowledge. Your fight-or-flight response, reflexive actions, and other instinctual behaviors all generate from this part of your brain.

2. **Limbic.** Your limbic brain sits on top of your reptilian brain and most likely developed as man evolved. It helps you focus on your emotional life and the formation of memories. Your limbic system contains structures responsible for sensations of pleasure and pain, happiness and fear, and is very responsive to hormones and drugs, such as opiates like morphine. Limbic structures become highly activated when you dream. Your limbic system provides the gateway to the formation of powerful, emotional memories and compels you to seek sensations that make you happy or fill you with pleasure.

3. **Neocortex.** This is your "higher" brain. It's the part of the brain you have seen a million pictures of because it sits on top of and surrounds your limbic brain; it resembles a gelatinous wrinkled mushroom cap.

Wrinkles Are Beautiful

When you look at pictures of the brain, one of the things you'll notice first is that the surface of your neocortex is covered with what appear to be wrinkles. These wrinkles aren't signs of age; they're an evolutionary adaptation. Having wrinkles and folds in the surface of your brain allows for the surface area to be many times larger than it would be if your brain was smooth; the wrinkles allow us to pack many millions more neurons within our skulls. They let us make more neuron associations and give us a great ability to learn and make new connections as we age.

The neocortex is also responsible for planning, abstract thoughts, and reasoning. It's the part of your brain that senses and perceives the world around you, allows you to formulate reactions, and allows you to think about thinking. Your personality, your hopes, and even your ability to speak all generate from—and reside within—your neocortex.

Visualize This!

To get a visual idea of the size of your brain, put your two palms together and then make your hands into fists. When you look down at your thumbs, you can see the approximate size of your brain. Your curled up fingers even look a bit like the wrinkles in the surface of your brain. Its 100 billion nerve cells weigh about three pounds in total and connect with each other along 100 trillion different pathways.

THE FIVE MAJOR AREAS OF YOUR CORTEX AND THEIR FUNCTIONS

Because your cortex surrounds and covers your reptilian and limbic brains, a surgeon would have to remove this part of the brain, or cut into it, in order to see many of the other structures underneath. It's so large and contains so many of your highest-order functions that neuroscientists have divided the neocortex into four lobes (based on the type of information each manages) and the cerebellum, or "little brain."

1. Your frontal lobe
2. Your temporal lobe
3. Your parietal lobe
4. Your occipital lobe
5. Your cerebellum

These lobes are divided into left and right halves, or hemispheres, by the central sulcus, which runs lengthwise down the center of your brain. For the most part, the left and right halves of these lobes are responsible for similar functions, but each focuses on opposite sides of your body. The left side of your brain is concerned with the right side of your body, and the right side of your brain is responsible for the left side of your body.

In addition to these four cerebral lobes, many neuroscientists also include the cerebellum—literally your "little brain"—as a fifth major area.

Yes, it's complicated, but hang in with us as we describe what each area of your brain does. Getting to know the parts of your brain will vastly improve your ability to understand how it functions overall and what you can do to protect and improve your brain functions and thereby increase your level of happiness!

Your Frontal Lobe

At the very front of your brain lies an area known as the frontal lobe. It is the largest of the lobes—about 30 percent of your brain's overall size—and is the most highly evolved portion of your brain. It is the frontal lobe that makes us human. It controls most of your executive decision-making, serves as the seat of your personality, and is the part of your brain that allows you to think about yourself. Some call the frontal cortex "the CEO of your brain" because it is responsible for double-checking decisions and actions and giving the final okay before you interact with the rest of the world.

Your Prefrontal Cortex

At the heart of the frontal lobe is an area known as the prefrontal cortex (or PFC), which is likewise divided into left and right halves, or hemispheres. The left part of your PFC is concerned with emotional responses, while the right half of your PFC is more concerned with fact-based analysis. The PFC sits directly behind the center of your forehead and is the last to develop as you grow into an adult. Although teenagers like to think they have fully formed brains, the prefrontal cortex is still growing and doesn't really begin to shine until postadolescence. On average, this process begins and finishes about a year earlier in girls as compared to boys.

Why Teenage Couch Potatoes Get Even Lazier

A research group at the National Institutes of Health in Bethesda, Maryland, hypothesizes that the growth and changes in prefrontal cortical connections in teens is a particularly important stage of brain development. What teens do or do not do has the potential to affect them for the rest of their lives. This hypothesis is known as the "use it or lose it principle." If a teen is doing music, sports, or academics, those are the cells and connections that will be wired well as the prefrontal cortex matures. If they're lying on the couch or playing video games all day, those connections are going to survive and feel rewarding, and it will be harder to develop skills related to more active pursuits as habits need to be changed. What you choose to do in your adolescence—and in your adult years—*can* change your brain, for better or worse!

This prefrontal cortex serves as the integration center of all of your brain-mind functions. In other words, it not only regulates the signals that your neurons transmit to other brain parts and to your body, but it allows you to think about and reflect upon what you are physically doing. In particular, the PFC allows you to control your emotional responses through connections to your deep limbic brain. It gives you the ability to focus on whatever you choose and to gain insight about your thinking processes. The PFC is the only part of your brain that can control your emotions and behaviors and help you focus on whatever goals you elect to pursue. It helps you grow as a human being, change what you wish to change, and live life the way *you* decide!

The Temporal Lobe

As the name suggests, the temporal lobe is the part of your brain that resides under your temples on either side of your head, just behind and below the frontal cortex (thus, there are actually two separate temporal cortices). Your temporal lobes provide some sensory processing, most notably hearing, and contains the areas of your brain that are responsible for both speaking and understanding speech. However, each of the temporal lobes also houses its attendant hippocampus (again, there are two of them, one on each side, and the plural term is "hippocampi." However, here we'll just refer to "the hippocampus" and incorporate both structures into this definition). Your hippocampus converts short-term memories into long-term memories for storage and is critical for the formation of new factual or emotional experiences. Alzheimer's plaques, for example, begin in the cortex near the hippocampus and then enter the hippocampus. Memory loss is often the first sign of Alzheimer's disease.

Phineas Gage: The Man Who Lost His Prefrontal Cortex

Phineas Gage was a quiet, respected railroad construction foreman who, in 1848, was impaled with a railroad spike after an unexpected explosion at his work site. This spike pierced his left eye and came out the top of his head, destroying his prefrontal cortex but leaving the rest of the brain unharmed. Remarkably, Gage was not killed, nor even knocked unconscious from this ordeal. However, after recovery from the wound, he became an entirely different man, going from happy to rude, from hardworking to impulsive and brash. However, poor Phineas's injury helped neuroscientists realize the importance of the prefrontal cortex in developing personality, emotional control, and the ability to make and follow complex rules.

Your temporal lobe serves as the gateway to thoughts and experiences and determines how they are processed and stored in your mind. Many mood disorders emerge from the dysfunction of the temporal lobe and the inability to process memories correctly. A fully functioning temporal lobe makes for a happier you!

The Parietal Lobe

The two halves of your parietal lobe rest at the top of your brain, just behind your frontal lobe and above your temporal lobes. This parietal lobe handles the bulk of sensory integration, receiving information from different types of sensation—like touch and vision—and creating a smooth data stream that works together in real time. Your parietal lobes provide your sense of where you are in the world (known to neuroscientists as *proprioception*). It basically helps you navigate your way through your day-to-day life without bumping into walls.

Einstein's Brain: Changes Equal Processing Power

Albert Einstein's brain was preserved for many years after his death. Upon examination, neuroscientists discovered that the world's most famous genius experienced different changes in his brain from most other brains. Notably, the area that separated his temporal lobe from his parietal lobe was almost completely gone, and neuroscientists believe that this could account for his more integrative way of thinking and his ability to make unusual associations that other, "more normal" people couldn't see. A researcher from the University of California–Berkeley also found that Einstein had more brain connections in these "logical" brain parts than other men. Einstein's brain shows us that changing your connections, and the structure of your brain, really *can* help you think differently, more clearly, and with more clarity!

Your parietal lobe is also where knowledge and reasoning concerning numbers takes place. Many neuroscientists agree that, since many types of fact-based senses are integrated in the parietal lobes (i.e., *where* you are in the world, *what* you are looking at, *how* you are going to make an action to respond), this lobe is concerned with the logical aspects of interacting with the world and is less concerned with emotional responses.

The Occipital Lobe

The two halves of the occipital lobe sit at the rear of your brain, just behind and below the parietal lobes, at the back of your head. This part of the brain is concerned with processing all of the visual information coming into your brain from your eyes. Since we humans tend to rely on our vision more than any other senses, we have an entire lobe of the brain dedicated to processing detailed visual information.

The Cerebellum

Your cerebellum, often referred to as your "little brain," sits underneath the occipital lobes and parietal lobes and is a distinctly different cluster of cells that are separate from your four neocrotical lobes. Fully 50 percent of all of the brain's neurons are packed into this little region, which is important in motor control, your ability to pay attention, and experiencing basic emotional responses, such as fear and pleasure.

Much of the cerebellum's input is centered upon fine-tuning your actions to the outside world, making sure that you walk in a straight line or grasp your fingers with the right amount of pressure around a delicate eggshell, for example. It computes a lot of information in a very small space, and recently neuroscientists have come to realize that the cerebellum is also pivotal in other learning processes, most of which are largely subconscious. A professional baseball player moving his hand to catch a line drive uses his cerebellum much in the same way that you respond to a sudden, loud sound by reflexively jumping. Both of these responses arise from action patterns embedded in the cerebellum, as do many of your basic emotional responses.

DEEPER BRAIN STRUCTURES

The neocortex is large and imposing, and the many functions it handles are the ones that are most instantly recognizable:

- It is important for how we think about ourselves and connect to the outside world.
- It contains all the functions we recognize as distinctly human: language, the ability to think and reason, verbal communication, complicated learning, and abstract thinking.

However, the neocortex only makes up one-third of your brain, and the many parts that lie underneath it hold the key to some of our most important functions. These structures are usually known as "deep" brain areas, since you need to "dive" under the neocortex in order to find them. Most of the areas of your limbic system, or emotional brain, are located in these deep places.

Anterior Cingulate Cortex

The name of this brain region is a mouthful (as was its former name, anterior cingulate gyrus), but it describes exactly where it is and what it looks like. "Anterior" indicates that it is close to the front of the brain, located just behind your frontal lobes. "Cingulate" is Latin for "belt" and thus describes how this region "wraps around" another deep brain structure called the corpus callosum. "Gyrus" originated from the Latin word *gyre*, meaning a circle or turning. Taken together, this accurately describes this brain region as a forward area that surrounds other, lower brain structures and is turned or bent like a fold.

The anterior cingulate cortex is situated right between the decision-making frontal cortex and the emotional limbic brain, where it performs as an emotional gear-shifter. It brings information concerning emotions, empathy, and reward from the lower limbic brain structures to the prefrontal cortex. Once the information is processed in the prefrontal cortex, a reaction to the information and a plan for action is delivered back down through the anterior cingulate cortex to the limbic brain.

Why Being Happy Matters

Being happy matters more than you might think. Feeling pleasure can be very stimulating for your brain, so much so that your brain is primed to respond to pleasure in a way that reinforces pleasure. Other than being much more fun to be around, here are a few reasons why being happy matters, particularly in relation to your brain's health:

- Happiness stimulates the growth of nerve connections.
- Happiness improves cognition by increasing mental productivity.

- Happiness improves your ability to analyze and think.
- Happiness affects your view of surroundings.
- Happiness increases attentiveness.
- Happy thoughts lead to more happy thoughts.
- Happy people are more creative, solve problems faster, and tend to be more mentally alert.

Thus, emotional information is ramped up or ramped down depending on the amount of information passing through this cortex. By learning to strengthen your prefrontal cortex's ability to control emotional responses, you can train your brain to increase the neuronal connections sent back down to suppress unwanted or negative emotional states arising from the deeper limbic structures. Achieving this will allow your brain to shift more easily into higher gears of happiness.

The Deep Limbic System

Sharing a connection to the anterior cingulate cortex, this walnut-sized area contains the thalamus, hypothalamus, and the amygdala. Each performs important functions:

- **Thalamus:** Located at the top of the brain stem, it relays messages from the spinal cord up to the cerebrum and back down the spinal cord to your nervous system.
- **Hypothalamus:** Located directly below the thalamus, it maintains many of your body's hormones and monitors bodily functions, like blood pressure, body temperature, body weight, and appetite.
- **Amygdala:** Lies deep in the center of your limbic brain and is the size of an almond. It is in charge of many basic and emotionally charged needs, including love and sex. It triggers strong emotions, like anger, fear, love, lust, jealousy, and so on. More recently, it has been connected to depression and even autism. It's often slightly larger in males, enlarged in sociopathic brains, and diminishes slightly in size as you age.

Your deep limbic system is an older part of your mammalian brain, which was the first to enable animals and humans to experience and express emotions. It is responsible for passion, emotion, and desire, all of which add emotional spice to our lives in both positive and negative ways.

In general, when your deep limbic system is quieted, or less active, you experience a positive, more hopeful state of mind. When your deep limbic system is heated up, or overactive, negativity can take over. This emotional coloring of events is critical, as the importance you give to events in your life drives you to action (such as avidly pursuing something that makes you happy) or causes avoidance behavior (withdrawing from something that has scared or hurt you in the past).

Limbic Brain: It's All about Love, Baby

Your ability to offer nurturance, social communion, and playful interactions generates in your limbic brain. Studies have found that removing a mother hamster's entire neocortical [higher] brain will not affect her ability to take care of her children, but if her limbic brain suffers even slight damage, she loses all ability to love and nurture her children.

Basal Ganglia

Your basal ganglia are a series of brain areas, or "nuclei," that are classified into two sets that serve distinct functions:

1. The first set (consisting of the striatum, pallidum, substantia nigra, and subthalamic nucleus) is concerned with motor control. Currently, these basal ganglia regions are thought to be primarily involved with action selection, that is, making a quick decision between several possible reaction plans; for instance, deciding to take a quick step left if someone is riding a bike

toward you on the pavement, rather than stepping backwards or doing a somersault.

2. The second set, collectively known as the limbic nuclei of the basal ganglia, consists of the nucleus accumbens, the ventral pallidum, and the ventral tegmental area. These three areas play an important role in determining sensations of reward and anxiety, particularly via the connections between the ventral tegmental area and the nucleus accumbens. Many addictive drugs, such as cocaine, amphetamines, and nicotine, affect this pathway, as do more natural rewards like savoring excellent food and enjoying sex.

Basically, if it feels good and makes you happy, your second set of basal ganglia are being excited. Stimulating this pathway by any rewarding behavior, or associating a reward with a particular place or mood, can help you take the driver's seat when it comes to feeling happy, or feeling anxious.

Too Much of a Good Thing?

The reward connection between the ventral tegmental area and the nucleus accumbens is one of the most powerful pleasure pathways in the brain, and it is highly stimulated by addictive drugs such as cocaine. Laboratory rats given free access to cocaine and taught to inject themselves with the drug by pressing a lever will often choose to self-administer cocaine, even when given a choice between the drug and tasty food. In fact, some rats chose the drug over food until they reached the brink of starvation. Clearly, strong feelings of love, happiness, and pleasure can overpower even basic survival instincts, such as the need to eat.

NEUROTRANSMITTERS AND WHY THEY MATTER

Your brain consists of a network of neurons whose sole responsibility is to transmit signals from cell to cell. These signals are electrically transported within a single neuron and chemically transported between neurons. Neurotransmitters deliver the chemical messages. There are many different kinds of neurotransmitters, and thus they are able to transmit gradients of information more easily than a simple electrical signal. Some neurotransmitters deliver fairly straightforward, simple messages.

Other neurotransmitters are more complex and have different functions in different brain areas, and these types of neurotransmitters are often called *neuromodulators*. Three of the more well-known neuromodulators are dopamine, serotonin, and acetylcholine. Dopamine and serotonin, in particular, are known to be key neurotransmitters in the regulation of pleasure, happiness, reward, and mood. Acetylcholine has been shown to be important in shifting from sleep to wakefulness and helps in sustaining attention and forming memories, especially in the hippocampus.

Even small changes in the number of neuromodulators that transmit signals from neuron to neuron can have a noticeable impact on your mood, disposition, and thought processes. For example, many addictive drugs overstimulate the dopamine system and lead to abnormal behaviors, both during the high, when the addictive drug causes dopamine levels to soar, and during the low, when the addictive drug has been cleared from your system and dopamine levels subside.

Having too much or too little dopamine has also been implicated in behavior disorders from attention deficit hyperactivity disorder (ADHD) to schizophrenia. Changes in the balance of serotonin in your brain can also lead to mood disorders, such as clinical depression, anxiety attacks, and phobias. Thus, having the right balance of neurotransmitters allows for your brain to hum along, operating at its full capacity with *you* in control.

NEURAL PATHWAYS TO HAPPINESS

Every thought, perception, sensation, and emotion that expresses "you" has an electrical and chemical component: Genes, neuronal impulses, and neurotransmitters combine to express your personality as a sort of cocktail of emotional responses, drives, and memories. This cocktail settles your brain into patterns, and often into habits. Habit forms a brain pathway simply because that particular neuronal pathway has been stimulated many times, usually because the original stimulation was perceived as positive. Habits effectively become a kind of addiction—an electrochemical itch that you feel compelled to scratch.

If you want to form new habits or discard old ones, you will have to consciously forge new, positively affiliated connections between the emotional limbic parts of your brain and your executive, or controlling, prefrontal cortex. Getting old neuron networks and new neuron networks—and the neurotransmitters associated with them—to work together to form smoother pathways often requires stimulating the brain with different activities, or different levels of activity, which we will discuss throughout this book.

Different levels of activity are usually characterized as brain waves, which are pulses of activity that are occurring at regular intervals. Certain types of brain waves are associated with different electrochemically active states and complexity of thinking.

Beta Brain Waves

The mental activity normally associated with beta waves is the active awareness state that we experience from day to day at work and play. Beta brain waves kick in when you think logically, solve problems, and confront external stimuli. Beta brain waves have the ability to increase muscle tension, raise blood pressure, and create anxiety. It is not a state used in quiet reflection, but rather a state for getting things done. Dopamine is released more easily when your brain is in a beta frequency.

Alpha Brain Waves

These are the opposite of beta brain waves; alpha waves are prominent during relaxation, especially when your eyes are closed. Your brain moves in an alpha rhythm when you are daydreaming or in a state of introspection. Alpha waves stimulate an increase in melatonin, which is a chemical often associated with sleepiness.

Theta Brain Waves

Theta brain waves engage inner and intuitive subconscious. You'll find that your brain waves are in a theta frequency when you are going through memories or experiencing strong sensations and emotions. Theta waves are also found when we are storing secrets, which we block out in times of pain, to survive what we feel unprepared to fix. Theta brain waves are often engaged when you sleep and are the equivalent of flexing emotional and dreaming brain muscles. People who have brain waves that often border between theta and beta frequencies are usually reported to be very extroverted and have low anxiety and low neuroticism: They seem to have found the balance between emotional and active, logical thinking. The neurotransmitter serotonin is often associated with theta brain waves, as is the neurotransmitter GABA (gamma-aminobutyric acid).

Delta Brain Waves

These are slower brain waves often associated with unconscious feelings and empathy. In healthy doses, these signals cause the right amount of empathy, but too much delta activity can force you to forget about yourself and your needs. Delta waves are the least well studied of the brain wave states, even though they are often associated with higher levels of serotonin.

Gamma Brain Waves

Gamma waves are without a doubt the fastest of the brain waves, operating at a frequency of 25–100 Hz (although usually found around 40 Hz). Neuroscientists only discovered them fairly recently, when those studying the visual system found that two unconnected neurons seemed to start to fire in time when an oscillation of about 40 Hz was reached. This is similar to a jazz musician playing a saxophone solo and another musician playing a different tune on the piano coming together to start playing the same notes, at the same time, in synchronized tandem. The more powerful the gamma wave, the more precise is the synchronization. Your brain areas—or your entire brain—in a gamma wave state tend to fire networks and form associations more quickly than a brain in any other state.

Why Television Turns Your Brain to Mush

Psychophysiologist Thomas Mulholland found that after just *thirty seconds* of watching television, your brain begins to produce alpha waves, which indicate slow rates of activity. Alpha brain waves are associated with unfocused, receptive-only states of consciousness, which mean watching television represents one of the few instances in which you can achieve an alpha brain wave state with your eyes open. Basically, watching television is neurologically analogous to staring at a blank wall or sitting with your eyes closed, doing—and thinking—absolutely nothing.

The formation of *gamma wave networks* could provide a vital clue as to how your brain may be able to change itself. When firing at an optimal speed, connections are formed more easily in an active mind. Allowing your brain to reach a gamma state could provide vital insights into how your brain can change itself, and how *you* can control the way in which it changes.

For example, during mindfulness meditation, monks far exceeded normal subjects when it came to the ability to generate intense, prolonged gamma wave activity in their prefrontal cortex, particularly on the left side. As we now know that the prefrontal cortex sits in the executive chair of the mind, generating gamma wave activity in this area would allow for precise connections to be formed between the part of your brain that allows you to control your behavior and the more emotional, subconscious parts of your deeper limbic system.

Thus, stimulating your brain into the highest levels of activity through concentrated mindfulness, and focusing on yourself, your actions, and your reactions, could allow you to produce a state whereby the brain has the best chance to change into what *you* want it to be—healthier, faster, and overall happier with your life.

THE ROLE OF GENETICS

For many years, scientists believed that your genetics—the information contained in your DNA—determined at least 50 percent of your happiness levels, while external factors like income, religion, marital status, and education accounted for only about 8 percent. The rest, they postulated, was up to chance, incidental factors, and vicissitudes—the things that happened to you in life—and your reaction to them.

However, more recent research by Richard Davidson, PhD, has placed DNA factors for happiness at closer to 30 percent. What is key to this brain plasticity—the near-miraculous ability to grow and change how your brain functions—is achieving a new focus and a new way of thinking. When you are able to see viable alternatives to what you perceive as limiting ways of thinking and acting, and are able to consciously adapt your thought patterns and behaviors, you will, over time, positively affect and change your brain's neural pathways and neurotransmitters.

Engaging the specific areas of the brain that are responsible for happiness—your left prefrontal cortex, your anterior cingulate cortex, and your deep limbic structures—will provide a map for your pathways to happiness. By utilizing techniques such as focused concentration, mindfulness meditation, and behavioral adaptation (all of which we'll be discussing in later chapters), you can strengthen the neuronal connections focused on positive emotions and lower your emotional responses to the negative, anxiety-ridden pathways that are likely undermining your ability to live a happy, fulfilling life.

Now that your brain is fired up and ready, all you have to do is start the engine . . . *and get your mind on board.* More about that in the next chapter!

CHAPTER 3

MIND OVER (GRAY) MATTER: The Difference Between Your Mind and Your Brain

"We should take care not to make the intellect our god; it has, of course, powerful muscles but no personality. It cannot lead; it can only serve."

—Albert Einstein

One of the oldest precepts of neuroscience has been that our mental processes (thinking) originate from brain activity—that our brain was in charge when it came to creating and shaping our mind. However, more recent research has shown that it can also work the other way around: that focused, repetitive mental activity can affect changes in your brain's structure, wiring, and capabilities. So, you may find yourself wondering: *Exactly what is the difference between my mind and my brain?*

THE DIFFERENCE BETWEEN YOUR BRAIN AND YOUR MIND . . . AND YOUR *SELF*

Because we are so used to (somewhat lazily) assuming that the mind and the brain are basically one and the same, it's not easy to explain. Let's begin by defining the three most important elements to this discussion in the simplest possible way:

1. **Brain:** An organ composed of soft nervous tissue that resides at the top of your spinal vertebrae (within the confines of your skull) and serves as your body's control central. It receives, processes,

and coordinates internal and external sensory information. It also serves as the repository for memories.

2. **Mind:** The element that allows a person to be aware of the world and his or her (internal and external) experiences in the world. The mind is the locus of consciousness and thought. Without a mind, you would not be able to think or to feel sensations or emotions.

3. **Self:** A person's essential being, the part of oneself that distinguishes that person from others, and all humans from animals. This is the locus of introspection, the element that allows a person to reflect upon his or her being.

Your Very Own Computer

Another way to understand the constructs, uniqueness, and interaction of brain, mind, and self is to envision the workings of a computer. Your brain would be what is hard-wired, the motherboard, if you will. Your mind would be the software, programs composed of your working knowledge of the world and how those programs interact with each other. Your self would be the content that the *you* in you types on the screen, the words and thoughts that arise from the interaction of your software (mind) with your motherboard (brain).

How Do Americans Compare to the Rest of the World?

According to a *Time* magazine article on happiness, when identical happiness polls were conducted in various countries throughout the world, Americans came out fifth in terms of happiness, thirty-third in terms of smiling, and tenth in terms of life enjoyment of life. At the same time, Americans were also the eighty-ninth most frequent worriers, the sixty-ninth saddest, and the fifth most stressed people. Still, perhaps because America is a relatively wealthy nation, we scored in the top ten citizenries where people feel their lives are going well, beaten out by such eternal optimists as the Canadians, New Zealanders, and Scandinavians.

In other words, thanks to the availability of the word processing software that you (consciously and unconsciously) installed on your motherboard—and their physiological interaction—your *self* generates the meaningful words that appear on the screen. *You* could type anything because the way that you use the software and the hardware is unique, and probably a little different from the way that anyone else would use it. Regardless of the words that you put on the screen, however, your self-created software (mind) functions by working in tandem with the hard-wired electronic circuitry of your computer's motherboard (brain).

Here's the most important part: Your software *instructs* your motherboard how to create the desired outcome. It's also important to note that detailed knowledge of the hardware (brain) is not really necessary in order to understand the software (mind) and vice versa. You don't need to know how your word processor interacts with the computer's memory system in order to use the tool. And both the hardware (brain) and the software (mind) are irrelevant to the content that arises from the self because the end user *(you)* utilizes the software and hardware the way that you need to use it. Minds are the products of brains, and selves depend on minds, but they require different forms of understanding.

Your Brain and Your Conscious Thought Process

Your brain performs certain essential tasks related to your conscious thought process. The various regions of your brain have very specific functions, and each serves the needs of your mind. Basically, your brain performs the following functions:

- It takes in sensory information from the internal (body) and the external (world) environment.
- It uses this information to make conditional rules about the environment(s).
- It uses these conditional rules to respond to later information from the internal and external environment by comparing new input against these pre-existing rules, which can lead to eventual changes in the external and the internal environment (i.e., through muscles and glands).

Your Mind and Your Conscious Thought Process

Your mind performs certain essential tasks related to your conscious thought process, such as:

- It speeds the power of electrical impulses in the brain.
- It keeps you awake and able to consciously process information from the external world.
- It keeps your consciousness aware of focused input in order to weigh in on the rules your brain is making and thereby process meditated reactions.
- It provides abstract and complex thinking—putting together pieces of information that may not be related according to your brain and make sense of them.
- It provides logic and reasoning across senses and perceptions.
- It contains what we humans like to call your "soul."

Your Gray . . . and White Anatomy

Your brain is often depicted as a three-pound ball of gray mush that has the consistency of something between Jell-O and tofu. And, in large part, that is true. In living tissue, the gray matter actually has a gray-brown color that comes from capillary blood vessels that feed the brain cells and neuronal cell bodies, which are naturally gray. Some parts of the brain also have neurons, called *white matter*, that are actually pinkish white due to something called a myelin sheath that insulates the brain cells. Mostly the white matter consists of long-traveling connections between one area of the brain and another. It is in the gray matter that the bulk of the exciting thinking and processing occurs, even if the color is a bit drab. A recent study from University of College, London, found that people with stronger introspective ability—who were good at thinking about thinking— have a higher volume of gray matter in the PFC.

How Your Mind Seizes Control

Systematic investigations over several decades have identified the relationship between many brain structures and mental functions. Scientists know what parts of your brain are important and necessary for identifying shapes, or faces, and so on. So, it is easy enough to make the pragmatic assumption that your brain *creates* your mind (much of the hardware must exist before the software can interact with it). There is no chicken-and-egg conundrum here: The brain came first!

However, after your mind first comes into existence, via the proper functioning of your brain, a curious thing happens: After its inception, the mind/brain interface operates bidirectionally. That is, if a change is made at the level of your mind, and a desired outcome within your mind is reached, your brain *must* be involved. Brain functions maintain control of and drive mental activities. However, through using explicit mental activities, *you* can consciously seize control and drive brain functions and in turn create new mental activities and new brain functions.

So what is consciousness? Where does the *you* in you interact with the mind in this top-down process of self/mind/brain?

THE *YOU* IN YOU

Your autobiographical *self* (identity, personality) consists of biological processes constructed within your brain from numerous interactive components—neuronal connection by neuronal connection—over a period of time. These neuronal connections create a sort of brain map that your mind employs to form mental images.

This *you* in you is a uniquely human aspect of your being. It creates the more or less coherent picture of your history, a narrative with a lived past and an anticipated future. The narrative is constructed from real events, from imaginary events, and from past interpretations and reinterpretations of those events. What you perceive as your unique personality and identity emerges from your autobiographical self. And because you don't grow up in a vacuum, your autobiographical self is greatly affected by—and thereby incorporates—the culture (and family, and country) in which your accumulated interactions took place.

What Does It Mean When You Don't Feel Like Yourself?

We all use that excuse for acting grumpy or sad, but of course you are always *you*. It's just that you are not feeling, thinking, and acting in alignment with what you regard as most typical of you (or perhaps with what you wish was most typical of you, or with what you want others to perceive as the ideal you). In fact, your autobiographical self (personality, identity) is not written in stone. Your brain calls upon your cerebral cortex and your brain stem to stitch together the *you* that you'll be taking into the world each and every day.

Most of us—for better or worse—develop very stable, consistent, and largely predictable personalities. Some, however, never quite lock in to one distinct, predictable personality. In essence, they create permeable or flexible personalities, which can be lucky if they become brilliant artists or musicians or architects who can think outside the box and thus achieve wealth, fame, and fulfillment. This can prove somewhat unlucky for these individuals if they also have erratic quirks or temperaments that are felt and perceived as unstable, unpredictable, and antisocial.

The Positive Psychology Philosophy

In order to more fully understand what creates "authentic happiness," Martin Seligman, PhD, founder of Positive Psychology (and author of *Authentic Happiness*), studied more than 200 books written over the last 3,000 years—everything from Aristotle to Aquinas, the Old Testament, the Koran, and the writings of Benjamin Franklin. He concluded that authentic happiness comes from using our inherent, signature strengths (inborn talents or psychological characteristics) to execute positive, meaningful action. When positive action or emotions are alienated from the exercise of your characteristic strengths, Seligman believes it results in feeling inauthentic or empty.

HOW ARE MEMORIES FORMED?

Because your thoughts and your thinking processes generate from your unique life experiences—and how you learn to think and feel about them—your personality emerges from your memories, how you felt about your memories, how you processed your memories, and so on. Your memories make you unique.

The Two Kinds of Memories

As a human, you have two kinds of memory, both of which affect how you think about your past, your present, and future events:

1. **Implicit memories** are unconscious emotional memories (sometimes called the "dark continent" or shadow brain). They consist of intuitive knowledge, feelings, and biases that we have no idea *how we know what we "know"* or how to access it consciously. Implicit memory contains silent, incremental knowledge that has nothing to do with facts, lists, or memorization. When it occurs, it makes language structures available for immediate use, but it's not so easily called up for reflection. Thus, unconscious (implicit) memories are those about which we may have no idea how we've acquired them or how to access them. These may include traumatic events that we've repressed, suppressed, or somehow have pushed out of our memory, but they also consist of physical learning, such as learning to talk, walk, or color. Because these activities occur while you are very young, you won't retain a memory related to the process of learning the

skill, only the ability to perform the skill. And if these skills are lost due to injury, you can train another area of your brain to perform these functions.

2. **Explicit memories** are gained from experience and thus are primarily conscious memories (unless we've forgotten certain details) that affect our view of ongoing events. These memories are generally readily available to us and are a product of past experiences, including how we've been parented, our family makeup, and all other environmental issues, such as location and culture. Explicit memories are very unique to each individual—even identical twins don't form the same explicit memories, as each has his or her unique own environments or experiences. Explicit memories generally serve themselves up for contemplation (the hippocampus is crucial to the creation and regeneration of explicit memories), but they can be unreliable. Studies have shown that memories change over time, partially due to aging or simply because nothing has stimulated that memory for a long time. We all rewrite history . . . so why not tweak your mental history to weaken the negativity and pain associated with past memories? We'll discuss techniques for doing this in the coming chapters.

Where Do Your Memories Live?

Different types of memories end up residing in different parts of your brain, for example:

- Learning that is concerned with facts—names, dates, events, *explicit* memories—result in memories that pass through your hippocampus and are primarily stored in your neocortex.
- Learning that has to do with skills or performing actions—such as playing the piano or using a tool, *implicit* memories—are usually stored in other brain areas, like your cerebellum.
- Emotional memories—things that make you happy, sad, or frightened—are a mixture of both types of memories. Emotional events are processed in sensory systems, such as vision or hear-

ing, and then simultaneously transmitted to the medial temporal lobe for the formation of an explicit memory about the facts of the situation that led to the emotion (where you were, who was with you) and to the amygdala and other limbic centers for the formation of the memory of the emotion associated with the facts. When a cue about the memory occurs and is processed by the sensory system, it leads to the retrieval of a fact-based, conscious memory about the emotional event but *also* leads to the expression of emotional responses when retrieved from limbic structures. In this way, emotions are transcendent—they have the ability to tap both explicit and implicit memory structures.

Why Connections Matter

The explicit facts associated with emotions can get parceled out by your neocortex, whereas the emotional component (implicit fear or happy response) of the memory gets stored in limbic systems. It's sort of like the memory gets separated into its building blocks, but those blocks are connected and can be put together to form a whole quickly depending upon the strength of the associated connection.

For many years, it was believed that once a memory link was formed, it was fairly immutable; the cellular changes within newly linked cells were thought to be irreversible after some six to twenty-four hours had passed. As late as 1992, a medical researcher named Daniel Alkon (who was among the first scientists to identify some of the cellular and molecular changes associated with memory) lamented that most memories of early painful abuse could, under this way of thinking, become permanent.

Patient HM

Henry Gustav Molaison (known to neuroscientists as simply "HM") began experiencing chronic temporal lobe seizures, originating from both of his hippocampi, at an early age. When his seizures became life threatening, in the 1950s, in a desperate move to save his life, neurosurgeons removed both of his hippocampi. Upon awakening, HM could no longer form new fact-based memories, and he could not commit any new ideas to long-term memory. However, he was able to make new *procedural* memories (skill-related memories), which allowed him to learn new motor skills such as drawing pictures. Because procedural memories don't rely on the hippocampus to become long-term memories, HM could draw without remembering having learned how to do so. Luckily, HM allowed researchers to study his brain for the next fifty years, and that research played a pivotal role in the development of theories that explain the link between brain function and memory. HM became one of the most famous neurosurgery patients of all time . . . if only he'd been able to remember it!

Reactivating Memories

We now know that some of these memories can possibly be modified and/or expelled with expert intervention. In fact, neuroscientists now theorize that memories have the ability to be modified each time they are actively recalled. For instance, exposure therapy has been effective in helping people suffering from particular, deep-set phobias neutralize the phobia by isolating the fearful component of their memory (whose initial association with the object or situation caused the phobic response) and working with the patients to reframe the memory, minus the emotional component.

Other research has shown that asking patients with posttraumatic stress disorder (PTSD) to recall their traumatic events, while their doctors simultaneously administer drugs that stimulate "calm" brain and body responses, will stop associating fear with the memory, untwining the emotional and factual events of their memory and making the negative emotional reaction lessen over time. It doesn't seem to matter how old the memory is; as long as it can be brought to the surface, it can be modified. All it takes is conscious thought and a desire to turn a negative into a positive, or at least a neutral, experience.

False Memories: Did You Remember to Turn Off the Oven?

There have been many studies about the phenomenon of "false memories," defined as remembering something that never actually happened. Scientists at the University of Muenster in Germany have shown that up to 25 percent of people will remember doing something themselves that, in reality, they merely saw someone else do—such as locking a door or shuffling a deck of cards—up to two weeks after the observation occurred. This may be due to a stimulation of neurons that would represent performing the action in your own brain and thus could activate motor representations similar to those produced when you perform an action yourself.

UNDERSTANDING HOW YOUR BODY AND YOUR BRAIN EXPERIENCE HAPPINESS

To create more happiness in your life, you first need to understand how your body and your brain perceive and experience happiness. Basically, your body gets the ball rolling, because your brain relies on your body for information. What your body encounters or senses or experiences is communicated to your brain, then your brain responds electrically, chemically, and, if necessary, physically.

Your Nervous Systems

Let's backtrack one step to explain your body's nervous system. For the purposes of delivering information to your brain, your nervous system has two components:

1. **Voluntary or somatic nervous system.** This system consists of the nerves that are ultimately connected to the "thinking" parts of your brain in the neocortex (remember, this is where your thoughts and imagination arise). Your brain responds by issuing commands to move certain muscles or initiate responses from your glands. While many of your muscular movements become so rote you aren't aware of consciously issuing executive orders to your muscles to perform them (for instance, walking, tying your shoes, typing), they are, in fact, controlled by your voluntary nervous system in response to your needs or conscious requests. When you have to relearn how to walk after an accident, you become much more conscious of how your voluntary nervous system functions.

2. **Involuntary or autonomic nervous system.** This system consists of the nerves that travel from sensory organs and the spinal cord to your brain stem and other lower-brain areas that control involuntary physical functions, such as your heartbeat, breathing, and digestion. This system controls our unconscious physical responses to stimuli, such as our hearts racing, our palms sweating, and our breathing growing shallow. These involuntary responses are our body's way of alerting us to a multitude of situations, everything from danger to love.

Your autonomic nervous system relieves your brain of the necessity to focus on the millions of minute tasks required for you to live and to move about in the world. (Imagine how little you'd get done if you had to think about breathing!) It works in tandem with your brain by sending and receiving electrical signals via the nervous system and chemical messages via hormones, and it all functions beautifully—unless something is drastic enough to upset the apple cart. That something could range from the development of a physical illness, such as diabetes, or from something you encounter in the world, such as an incredibly attractive person. In both cases, your autonomic nervous system sends messages to your brain that something has to be done!

How Do Emotions Fit In?

Emotions are an energetic expression (thanks to your autonomic nervous system) of how your physical body is experiencing a situation. In the case of a handsome stranger, your heart might involuntarily race or your face might flush. Those physical messages travel from your autonomic nervous system to your lower limbic brain, which then communicates the visceral response to your thinking brain, the neocortex, which would likely let you know fairly quickly that you're feeling very attracted to this person—and perhaps issue a directive to smile or wink.

Anxiety Is a Different Kind of Emotion

Two almond-sized organs, known collectively as your amygdala, are tucked deep into your brain and technically cause anxiety. When a threat is imminent, your sensory organs send alarm messages to your amygdala, which then send messages to your neocortex that alert it to danger. Soon you are in full-blown flight-or-fight mode, with adrenaline flooding into your muscles and your heart pumping in anticipation of a need to react. For most people, when the threat subsides, so does the alarm, which calms your amygdala back down to normal. Some people, however, continue to perceive threats when they no longer exist. Unfortunately, this causes a great deal of stress, inducing the release of the stress hormone cortisol. Having a lot of cortisol in the blood for a long period of time leads to physical symptoms, such as high blood pressure. It can also lead to psychological problems, such as post-traumatic stress disorder (PTSD), obsessive-compulsive disorder (OCD), and panic attacks.

Zen Baby: The Ultimate Beginner's Mind

Babies have more brain cells and fewer inhibitory neurotransmitters than grownups. As you grow up, your brain undergoes a pruning process that narrows your perception of life, which can lead to limited creativity and decreased ability to problem-solve. This pruning also limits your ability to be in the now and leaves you less open and less flexible. According to Alison Gopnik, author of *The Philosophical Baby*, a baby's brain, on the other hand, has an amazing, almost supersonic ability to sort through lots of excess information and remain more receptive to discovering highly rewarding solutions or intriguing, innovative concepts. A baby's brain notices the beauty and wonder around it and lives, very much, in the now. Babies have the ultimate "beginner's mind," which is so prized in Buddhism.

Are Emotions Conscious or Unconscious?

Emotions are unconscious until your brain processes the physical responses and *experiences them as feelings*. Thus, emotions are neither negative nor positive. They are simply designed as a system to attach significance to an inward or outward event, to let you know that something is out of the ordinary and that you should pay attention and respond. Emotions are your body's way of telling your brain that a situation is new, or dangerous or pleasurable—or anywhere in between. Emotions reflect neural excitement (created by input from your sensory organs) that builds to a crescendo, enters your awareness, creates feelings, and then declines.

Emotions Give You a Roadmap

Here are a few more insights about emotions that will help you in your quest to get happy:

- Emotions provide information designed to nudge you into action.
- Emotions can be altered through adaptive behaviors.

- Emotions help you know when you are in alignment with your needs and values, when you are feeling loved, when your needs aren't being met, when you are in danger, etc.

What's most important to remember is that your mind determines whether you view what caused the emotions as negative or positive. Painful emotions, such as feeling anxious, frightened, guilty, ashamed, angry, or overwhelmed, are simply calling your attention to the situation and urging you to either correct the situation or remove yourself from it. Positive emotions, such as feeling fulfilled, secure, joyful, confident, loved, or self-empowered, are reaffirming that your present situation is in alignment with your values and your healthy desires—that your needs are being met.

What Are Moods?

Moods are caused by sequential emotions, in the same tonal range, that don't ebb and flow, causing residual feelings that don't dissipate. Moods are also a state of enhanced readiness (anticipation) or preparation to experience a certain emotion. We fall into blue moods when sad feelings aren't resolved, the stimulus causing the sadness doesn't go away, or when we are fixated on pessimism. We feel joyful when things occur that create positive sensations, when we are anticipating something that we expect to be pleasant or rewarding, or because we are naturally upbeat and optimistic.

Emotions help you focus on what needs to be addressed to be happier. When you are emotionally unsettled, you can use that information to make adjustments that will bring you back into alignment with your higher self or your goals. Receiving and interpreting your emotions helps you root out the underlying problem—a person, place, or situation, but also stressful thoughts, limiting beliefs, or narratives you have going on in your mind.

Feelings Are Your Body's Response

Feelings are your *conscious experience* of emotional activation. You don't become aware of your feelings until your brain has processed all the sensations and perceptions and linked this new information to existing information. This happens, of course, at lightning speed; so fast that your feelings generally seem instantaneous. Like it or not, your brain is in control! Every feeling depends on your brain's ability to receive and process bodily sensations. This is why you can't just *decide* to be happy. Happiness is a *feeling* that arises out of a bodily experience; it's a result of receiving a sensation and how you perceive, or process, that information. The best you can do is strive to create situations that will lead to feeling safe, loved, energized, excited, fulfilled, joyful, and so on, and learn how to prevent those situations that lead to more negative emotions. You can change your environment (including who you come into contact with), your habits, the way you act (and, very importantly, *react* to the world), the way you think, and the way you *choose* to feel about past (and future) events. And, as this book proves, you can change your reactions, responses, and thought patterns by using your mind to train your brain to get happy.

When Feelings Lead You Astray

Your emotions and your feelings are both essential to your experience, but there are occasions when you shouldn't trust—or at least act upon—your feelings. Let's discuss a few:

- Your brain may have made connections early in your life relating one situation bluntly to another before it was capable of complex thinking or of perceiving the nuances of what occurred. This could cause you to react reflexively rather than appropriately to each new situation because of false impressions.
- You may feel highly aroused—in anger or in love—but it might not be the right time or place to express or act upon those feelings.
- You may be experiencing conflicting feelings, which may require time to sort out.

- You may be empathizing or reacting to the emotions, feelings, or moods of others around you and interpreting them to be your own, without realizing the source of the emotions or feelings.
- You may be under unusual stress due to a traumatic event, and your brain's chemistry will be in a stress mode and thus more likely to create feelings based on abnormal perception.

What's important is that you learn to monitor your emotions and use self-awareness to train your brain not to respond so reflexively.

OPTIMISM VERSUS PESSIMISM

Consistent, ongoing negative or positive feelings can have a great effect on your overall well-being. Neuroscientists have discovered that people who have a more cheerful disposition and are more prone to optimism generally show more brain activity in their left prefrontal cortex. Those who are less cheerful and lean more toward pessimism generally have more brain activity in their right prefrontal cortex.

Behaviors of Optimists and Pessimists

But that's a brain explanation. Behavioral scientists have observed very interesting differences between optimists and pessimists. In general, they have found that:

- Optimists attribute good events to themselves in terms of permanence, citing their traits and abilities as the cause, and bad events as transient (using terms such as "sometimes" or "lately" to describe them).
- Pessimists explain good events by citing transient causes, such as moods and effort, and bad events as permanent conditions ("always" or "never").

To get even more specific, they found that pessimists, for example:

- Automatically assume setbacks are permanent, pervasive, and due to personal failings.
- Are eight times more likely to be depressed than optimists.
- Perform worse at school and work.
- Have rockier interpersonal relationships.
- Die sooner than optimists.

Optimists, on the other hand:

- See setbacks as surmountable and particular to a single external problem, resulting from temporary problems or other people, not themselves.
- Lead happy, rich, fulfilled lives.
- Spend the least amount of time alone, and the most time socializing.
- Maintain healthier relationships.
- Have better health habits.
- Have stronger immune systems.
- Live longer than pessimists.

Emotional Balance

When positive and negative events happen, people usually experience a temporary burst of mood in one or the other direction. Over a short period of time, however, the emotional energy seeps out (an emotional osmosis of sorts), the person's mood settles back into its usual set range, and the person goes back to whatever is his/her "normal" level of happiness (or unhappiness). There is a rather famous study that showed that lottery winners experience the expected euphoria, but within a year of their win, they're back to being their usual self—whether or not they have lots of money left.

Optimism involves highly desirable cognitive, emotional, and motivational components. Optimists tend to have better moods, to be more persevering and successful, and to experience better physical health.

I Only Have Eyes for . . . *Me*

According to Sonia Lyubomirsky, a University of California researcher, unhappy people spend hours comparing themselves to other people, both above and below themselves on the happiness scale; happy people didn't compare themselves with anyone.

Which side would you rather play on? The good news is that you can use your mind to train your brain to tamp down the negative thoughts that lead to pessimism while ramping up the types of positive thoughts that lead to optimism. Even if depression runs in your family, you have the capability of improving the way your brain functions—of setting up neuronal roadblocks and diminishing the neuronal patterns linked to negative thinking. You may not be able to eradicate a genetic disposition toward depression, but you can greatly reduce its impact and its reoccurrence.

DOES YOUR MIND CONTROL YOUR BRAIN?

As we discussed in Chapter 1, thanks to modern technology that allowed neuroscientists to see with their own eyes how our brains work, scientific research has now proven that our brains are capable of neuroplasticity, or the ability to change itself, throughout our lifetimes. We are not stuck with the brain we were born with, and we have the ability to *consciously cultivate* (by using our minds) which parts of our brain we wish to strengthen, rewire, or even regenerate.

So, yes, it is possible for you to change connections between parts of your brain or shift mental activity from one region to the other. Indeed, the plasticity of your mind (its own ability to learn and adapt) arises from the ability of your neural connections to change.

How Using Your Mind Affects Your Brain

The act of thinking stimulates your brain by increasing blood flow to various regions of your brain (which brings additional glucose and oxygen to ramp up the electricity), bolstering or weakening existing neuronal synapses, and generating new neurons and synapses. In general, thinking affects your brain in the following ways:

- It sparks neuronal activity and thereby increases neuronal responsiveness to stimuli. The more you use your mind to study something, the more you strengthen the area of your brain related to that topic or skill.
- It increases blood flow, and thus brings additional glucose and oxygen to your neurons so they can function at a higher level—and form new synapses. Think of a region of your brain as a brightly burning fire that, when untended, slowly becomes embers. If you call upon your mind to think about certain subjects or tasks, it's like throwing gasoline on the fire, and new sparks can arise!
- It can cause neurons to fire together, which strengthens existing synapses and forms new ones. The neuronal activity feeds upon and strengthens itself. The more you think, the better you think.
- It has the potential to create neurogenesis, the birth of new neurons in your hippocampus. Yes, an old (human) dog *can* learn new tricks.

HERE'S A THOUGHT: USE YOUR MIND TO TRAIN YOUR BRAIN TO GET HAPPY!

So, can you really think your way to happiness? Aaron T. Beck, a leading cognitive theorist, would respond with a resounding, "Yes!" Beck, founder of cognitive behavioral therapy (CBT), which we'll discuss in depth in the next chapter, postulated that emotions and feelings are always generated by cognition (thoughts) and not the other way around, and he based his beliefs on observations that:

- Thoughts of danger lead to anger
- Thoughts of loss lead to sadness
- Thoughts of being wronged lead to anger

As we've learned, thoughts generate from both implicit memories (unconscious, preverbal memories) and explicit memories (conscious, remembered events). The way you think about these memories can have a tremendous effect on what happens in your life and how your brain works. Negative thoughts attract negative thoughts and potentially create a downward spiral into obsessive thinking and negative affect that could lead to a deep-seated depression. Positive thoughts, on the flip side, attract positive thoughts and flood your brain with a sense of well-being that will play a major factor in your level of happiness.

Most importantly, it has been widely shown that, over time, the way you choose to think can effect a noticeable change in your brain structure and how your brain operates.

So let's proceed to the next chapter, where we'll discuss specific techniques for using your mind to train your brain to get happier!

CHAPTER 4

THINK YOUR WAY TO HAPPINESS

"It isn't what you have, or who you are, or where you are, or what you are doing that makes you happy or unhappy. It is what you think about."

—Dale Carnegie

Now that you know how memories are formed and that thoughts arise from memories, it's time to discuss techniques for training your brain to get happy. Addressing the way you think sets the stage.

First, let's examine how your current thinking affects your happiness.

The Think Happy Quiz

1. When someone insults you, you react by:
   A. Shrugging it off and forgetting about it
   B. Replaying the scene over and over again but with your reacting differently
   C. Replaying the scene over and over again in your mind as it happened
   D. Plotting your revenge

2. When someone compliments you, you react by:
   A. Saying "Thank you"
   B. Trivializing it, as in "this old thing?"
   C. Questioning their motives
   D. Questioning their sanity

3. **You make a mistake at work. You:**
   A. Think of a solution and tell your boss
   B. Do nothing but worry about your boss finding out
   C. Think of a way to blame someone else
   D. Think you're going to be fired, so you quit

4. **Your lover breaks up with you. You:**
   A. Think there's something wrong with him/her
   B. Think there's something wrong with you
   C. Think all relationships are doomed
   D. Think all your relationships are doomed

5. **You find yourself feeling happy for no good reason. You:**
   A. Enjoy it
   B. Think something good is about to happen
   C. Think something bad is about to happen
   D. Chastise yourself for being silly

6. **When you have a bad day, you:**
   A. Acknowledge what's bothering you and let it go
   B. Acknowledge what's bothering you and obsess about it
   C. Distract yourself from your feelings by going to the movies
   D. Go to bed and stay there

7. **When you have a bad month, you:**
   A. Make a plan to change your life
   B. Take up a new hobby
   C. Resign yourself to feeling unhappy for a while
   D. Resign yourself to feeling unhappy forever

Now tally up your score.

- *If you checked mostly As,* you usually don't let your thoughts undermine your happiness for long. But there are still ways you can learn to alter your thought patterns to maximize your happiness.
- *If you checked mostly Bs,* you recognize that your thoughts can affect your moods, but you don't always succeed in keeping negative thought patterns at bay. Luckily, you can learn how to break the downward cycle of negative thinking more quickly so you can avoid the rut of unhappiness and reclaim a happier state sooner rather than later.
- *If you checked mostly Cs,* you often let your thoughts control your emotions—and not in a good way. This negativity affects your health and happiness, often in ways you're not even aware of. Once you recognize your ability to change the way you think about what happens to you, you can turn those thoughts from negative to positive—and become happier in the process.
- *If you checked mostly Ds,* you consistently allow your negative thought patterns to narrowly define your life—and thereby subverting your own happiness. Without rethinking your thought patterns, you will continue to sabotage your well-being—and ultimately, your potential for a happy and fulfilled life.

HOW THOUGHTS AND FEELINGS BECOME ENTRENCHED IN YOUR MIND

As you discovered in the previous chapter, many, if not all, of your emotions are a product of the way you perceive or interpret your environments; often these perceptions and interpretations are biased or distorted due to your moods.

Unfortunately, the way you think—or thought—about what happened can lead you to create unrealistic expectations or to harbor unreasonable and unsubstantiated concerns about your attractiveness, your intelligence, how others perceive you, and what you can achieve in the world. These negative connotations to your experiences—and the memories you have stored regarding them—often lead to distorted, biased, or illogical thinking processes that then affect how you feel about yourself and interact with others.

This then becomes your modus operandi—the way you are in your inner and outer world. *You are what you think*, basically. Unless you do something to shake things up, or unless something happens that shakes you up, your thought patterns can become entrenched, wearing a groove of habit and predictability in your brain.

On the flip side, if you've had a sunny life and a positive mindset, your memories are not as likely to be tarnished, and your thinking processes may be far healthier. But since most of us are coping with self-esteem issues that likely result from negative thoughts patterns—whether reinforced or newly sprung—we'll begin by discussing the dark side.

STINKING THINKING: HOW YOU GET STUCK IN NEGATIVE THOUGHT PATTERNS

Certain brain configurations cause people's emotions to repeat themselves, without decreasing substantially in intensity. In effect, their emotions don't turn off and thus give no respite to the poor soul attempting to cope with them. If the thoughts and feelings involve sadness or despair, the persistence can lead to depression, which digs in by blotting out any opposing feelings, thoughts, or motivation that could turn the tide. Manics get stuck in a similar way, just at the opposite end of the spectrum: feelings of euphoria that they have no control over.

Your Brain on Negative Thoughts

Negative thoughts will literally make your brain dysfunctional—in this case, that means function in a way that it was not designed to do. Prolonged negative thinking associated with depression causes emotional responses that are very hard to control. For example, in a recent study at the University of Wisconsin–Madison, both depressed and nondepressed adults were shown emotional pictures—such as scenes from a car accident—and were asked to consciously work to decrease their emotional responses to some of the negative images, using techniques such as envisioning a more positive outcome than the one implied, or by imagining the situation was acted out rather than real. These are techniques psychologists use to try and stem negative thinking and temper emotional responses.

In the nondepressed individuals, high levels of frontal and prefrontal activity correlated with low activity in their emotional response centers, such as the amygdala. In effect, the healthy subjects' efforts successfully quelled their emotional responses. In the depressed patients, however, high levels of activity in the amygdala, and other emotional centers, persisted despite intense activity in the regulatory regions. Researchers concluded that attempts by depressed people to suppress their negative responses actually backfire. Instead, they think even more negative thoughts.

This hardship in suppressing negative thinking may be due to changes in the brain associated with negative thought patterns. Dr. Husseini Maji of the National Institutes of Mental Health has noted brain atrophy in the hippocampus and the frontal lobes in patients suffering from depression. This atrophy (changes making these brain structures smaller) not only prevents new memories from being formed but weakens the ability of the frontal lobe to quiet the emotional reactions of the deep limbic structures. A smaller structure leads to fewer connections, making it that much harder to gain control over negative thought patterns.

Further, Dr. Luca Santarelli and Dr. Ronald Duman of Yale University led a team of scientists who showed that the reduction in connections is not necessarily because "old" brain cells are dying but, in fact, is because new cells—and therefore new connections!—are not being made at the same rate as they were in nondepressed persons.

Turning a Negative Into a Positive

Getting stuck in negative thought patterns makes it harder and harder for your brain to rebound by causing an overactive amygdala and a weakening in the prefrontal CEO of the brain, making it harder for the person to control these responses. With a smaller hippocampus, it also becomes harder to make new memories or change older, fearful ones.

Every moment that you can spend reversing negative patterns of thinking is important for getting your brain out of these patterns and into a happier, more productive state.

POSITIVE THINKING: HOW OPTIMISM SAVES THE DAY

Every thought releases brain chemicals. Being focused on negative thoughts effectively saps the brain of its positive forcefulness, slows it down, and can go as far as dimming your brain's ability to function, even creating depression. On the flip side, being focused on positive, happy, hopeful, optimistic, joyful thoughts produces chemicals that create a sense of well-being, which helps your brain function at peak capacity.

There are hundreds of benefits to being positive, among them: Being positive, especially around friends and family, will make it easier for them to do the same. So turn that frown upside down, and give your brain the juice it needs to function at its peak capacity, so you—and your brain—can feel good about life.

Your Brain on Happy Thoughts

"We choose and sculpt how our ever-changing minds will work, we choose who we will be the next moment in a very real sense, and these choices are left embossed in physical form on our material selves."

—Dr. Mike Merzenich

In contrast to the effects of negative thinking on your brain, positive thinking has really helpful effects on your brain. Happy thoughts and positive thinking in general seem to be responsible for the growth of the brain, making new synapses, especially in the prefrontal cortex (PFC). Neuroscientist Helen Mayberg used brain imaging to measure activity in the brains of depressed adults before they underwent fifteen to twenty sessions of behavior therapy, where they learned to reshape depressive thoughts. All the patients' depression lifted, and the only "drugs" that this group received were the own thoughts. She then scanned the patients' brains again. These scans reflected changed activity in both the limbic brain and the prefrontal cortex, showing without a doubt that the mind can change the brain, or as Dr. Mayberg explained, the mind can rewire the brain "to adopt different thinking circuits."

A Happy Brain Is an Energetic Brain

Negative thinking slows down brain coordination, making it difficult to process thoughts and find solutions. Feeling frightened, which often happens when focused on negative outcomes, has been shown to decrease activity in the cerebellum, which slows the brain's ability to process new information, and the left temporal lobe, which affects mood, memory, and impulse control.

So how do we think happy thoughts, even when feeling besieged by negative thoughts?

COGNITIVE BEHAVIORAL THERAPY TO THE RESCUE!

"As a man thinketh, so is he."

—Napoleon Hill

Cognitive behaviorism was formed as a reaction against the Freudian emphasis on consciousness as the subject matter and introspection as the method of its behavioral or therapeutic investigation. Freud believed that we experienced emotions first, and that our problematic thoughts arose from deep-seated emotions, many of which were repressed in our subconscious. Freud liked to delineate and probe his patient's psyche, hoping to ferret out suppressed fears.

In the early part of the twentieth century, American psychologist John B. Watson founded what became known as the psychological school of behaviorism, which basically rejected Freudian introspection and postulated that behavior should be the sole subject matter of psychology, and that it should be studied through simple observation.

In the 1970s and 1980s, American psychologist Aaron T. Beck shared Watson's dissatisfaction with traditional psychoanalysis and went a step further in postulating that "faulty learning"—that is, making incorrect inferences on the basis of inadequate or incorrect information, and not distinguishing adequately between imagination and reality—caused psychological disturbances. His theory led him to develop a method that became known as cognitive behavioral therapy (CBT), whose primary premise was that you (with or without a therapist) can work with thoughts and behaviors to change the way you cope psychologically.

Beck believed that distorted information processing—having unrealistic, negative views about yourself, the world, and your future—created the behavioral, affective, and motivational symptoms of depression and other psychological disorders. He believed that the healing process began with focusing on the cognitive content of your reaction to upsetting events or streams of thought. By scrutinizing the cognitive content and viewing it as a hypothesis rather than a substantiated conclusion, Beck believed the emotional reactions or problematic behaviors would subside. The more someone dealt with his or her ineffective or negative cognitive processing, the less he or she would focus on negative thoughts or memories, participate in rumination, or suffer emotional distress.

Overall, research based on the use of cognitive-behavioral interventions has demonstrated that CBT techniques are helpful in treating a large number of problems that we all encounter, as well as a wide range of more serious mental processing disorders, including:

- Depression
- Generalized anxiety disorder
- Panic attacks
- Posttraumatic stress disorder
- Social phobias
- Obsessive-compulsive disorders
- Some schizophrenic disorders

Dr. Amen's Research

Dr. Daniel Amen, neuroscientist, psychiatrist, and author of many books on how our brains work, is a big believer in "automatic negative thoughts," which are the self-defeating thoughts we can't control that crop up repeatedly in our day-to-day life, ones that we often *assume* to be correct. He noted in particular three types of automatic negative thoughts that trip up many a person:

1. **Thoughts of guilt:** "Oh, I should have done this" or "What I did was wrong."
2. **Negative mind-reading:** Negatively interpreting people's thoughts, or ascribing negative thoughts to them when they have not themselves said anything or even thought anything.
3. **Self-fulfilling fortune-telling:** Thinking, "I'm going to do badly on this test" followed by a failure to study, which negatively affects the outcome.

Dr. Amen believes one key to happiness is in recognizing and controlling these thoughts and not allowing our *selfs* (minds) to believe them.

HOW CBT WORKS

In its most basic formulation, CBT suggests that psychological distress is caused by distorted thoughts about stimuli that give rise to distressed emotions. As a therapeutic process, it focuses on breaking the cycle of unproductive thinking, as well as correcting errors in thinking. The theory is particularly well developed (and empirically supported) and has proven very useful in treating depression, where subjects frequently experience unduly negative thoughts that arise automatically, even in response to stimuli that might otherwise be experienced as positive. In depression research on the effectiveness of CBT, clients successfully treated with CBT have shown to experience half the relapse rate as people treated with antidepressant medication alone.

While CBT recognizes that family background, genetic and bio-chemical vulnerabilities, as well as numerous individual and social factors likely all play a role in how you think, feel, and act, the primary interest is in *determining the thoughts* that perpetuate the problems. In other words, it's not about delving into your past as much as it's about identifying negative thoughts that create distressing emotions or unproductive behaviors and then changing the thoughts or the thought process. The main focus is on helping to reduce the distress and related behaviors that are impairing a person's current functioning.

CBT approaches can be used to treat mood and anxiety disorders, eating disorders, relationship problems, anger and emotion regulation, personality disorders, and even substance abuse and psychotic disorders (the latter solely with professional help). The basic premise underlying CBT, whether it is conducted with an individual, family, couple, or in a group, is that thoughts, feelings, and behaviors are interrelated, so altering one can help to alleviate difficulties in another. For instance, changing negative thoughts about oneself can decrease "normal" feelings of sadness and anxiety, which ideally would improve your willingness to try new activities and work on improving relationships.

GENERAL CBT TECHNIQUES

CBT frees people from their past by getting them to change the way they think about it in the present and future. It uses many kinds of procedures to change negative or maladaptive kinds of thoughts. Here are four simple tactics you can use to change your negative thought patterns:

1. **Recognize conscious and uproot unconscious automatic thoughts,** particularly negative ones that keep your mind going in unproductive circles.
2. **Disperse these negative thoughts with contradictory evidence.** Support positive thoughts with validation and re-experiencing them, as needed.

3. **Create a different explanation to refute the original negative thought.** Argue with the part of yourself that believes the negative thoughts. And loosen up on being judgmental—of yourself and others.

4. **Employ distraction.** When all else fails, think about something else, or better yet, go do something physical and don't think at all until the negative thoughts subside.

USING CBT TO THINK YOUR WAY TO HAPPINESS

While Beck and his successors primarily work with patients in a therapeutic or clinical setting, it is very feasible for you to use CBT techniques as a way to improve your thinking. Basically, you want to work toward the following goals:

- Determine why you are feeling upset and/or behaving in an unhelpful way, that is, contrary to your goals.
- Evaluate your thinking to appraise situations and problems more realistically.
- Gain insight into why you think the way you do, addressing underlying beliefs about the way you see yourself, others, and your environment that are holding you back.
- Modify your thoughts and any unrealistic beliefs.
- Focus on positive self-affirmations to generate positive thoughts and positive action.

We'll outline the basics for how you can achieve these goals, and you can take it from there.

CBT Technique #1: Create a Self-Assessment Log

You may or may not be aware of your ongoing feelings and thoughts, how they are interlinked, and *why* you feel the way you do. Before beginning CBT, Beck had his patients pay attention to and track their thoughts and feelings in relation to what happened in their lives. He would instruct them to take a sheet of paper and title three columns: "Event," "Feelings," and "Thoughts," respectively. This method can work for you, too!

Simply create your chart and start paying attention. Keep these ideas in mind:

- Aim for recording at least three or four events each day, particularly those that have noticeable feelings and thoughts related to them.
- Pay particular notice to those that seem incongruous—for example, when your thoughts and feelings seem contrary, or out of proportion, to the event.
- Note recurring patterns, such as self-berating or punishing thoughts.
- Write down which of your thoughts lead to feelings of happiness or well-being.

After three or four days, review your list for patterns. You'll likely be able to identify some ongoing themes. This knowledge will help you see your thinking process, understand how your thinking affects your feelings, and create a new pathway for selecting CBT methods that will help you retrain your brain.

CBT Technique #2: Distract Your Thoughts

If you find it very difficult to stop thinking about your concerns, try this technique. It turns out that there is a limit to how many issues a person can be thinking about at the same time, which a University of Oregon study pegged as approximately four things. So if your negative thoughts are getting the better of you, add something positive to the mix to edge out the negative. Focusing on positive activities can give you welcome relief from an overly busy mind, as well as provide a haven from any continuing rumination upon self-defeating thoughts.

It's as simple as this: When a negative thought pops into your head, go do something else that will require you to think about what you are doing. Put together a complex puzzle; draw or paint (a picture, not a room); count the number of quarters you have stashed in your piggy bank and look up which ones are valuable; or write a long heartfelt letter, an essay, or a short story. *Do something* that requires concentration.

If you're someone who really gets into unproductive rumination, this technique can be a lifesaver—or at least a brain saver. The worst thing you can do is to become inactive. Idleness allows you to continue to think in a self-punitive manner, which opens the way for the onslaught of negative feelings to overwhelm you. Instead, keep those four available slots in your mind busy with positive thoughts.

CBT Technique #3: Try Guided Imagery

Two principles we mentioned briefly in preceding chapters make guided imagery an effective choice for training your brain to be happier. They are:

- Your brain cannot reliably distinguish between recorded experience and internal fantasy.
- New brain-scanning technology has shown that perception activates the same brain areas as imagination, indicating the possibility of transforming painful memories by employing active imagination.

Therefore, there is little doubt that guided imagery can be a powerful mood changer. Therapists often use it as a way for patients to revisit their past (both implicit and explicit memories), but you can also do this at home on your own.

Begin by drawing up a list of the most pleasant and enchanting experiences you've ever had, bringing all the delicious details to the front of your mind. Then get yourself as comfortable as possible in your favorite chair and take some slow, deep breaths to become even more relaxed. As you breathe slowly in and out, instruct your brain to stop thinking about the list of tasks you need to accomplish or worrying about something in your past or future. In other words, clear your mind of any distracting thoughts.

Next, select a pleasant experience from your list and slowly and vividly relive the related pictures and sounds. Close your eyes and re-experience every detail you can recall, including associated aromas and scents, as well as any tastes and tactile sensations connected to the memory. Linger in that recreation, picturing the scene so vividly in your mind that all the warmth and happiness washes over you, permitting you to truly take in each detail and each feeling anew.

How Do I Love Me . . . Let Me Count the Ways

Another version of using guided imagery involves creating a list of your strengths and associated successes, and then reading it daily for a few weeks or however long it takes for these positive self-affirmations to sink in. This exercise can act as a powerful mood changer as well.

You can also use this same technique to envision future events as a way of rehearsing for a future event. Simply use the same method to draw a picture in your mind of how you want the event to play out. Use sensate details to make it come alive in your mind, creating a palpable feeling of pleasant anticipation. Practice this often and well, and you will train your brain to zip down those neuronal pathways when the actual event comes around.

Now slowly bring yourself to the present by becoming centered again in your body, from the soles of your feet to the crown of your head. Take a deep breath and slowly open your eyes. You will likely feel rejuvenated and happy, and ready to focus on thinking happy thoughts.

Congratulations, you've just "tricked" your mind into reliving the event *as if it is happening again in reality.* This process can literally spark the existing neurons and strengthen the neuronal connections associated with the first memory, which essentially doubles your levels of pleasure and happiness. The more you remember happy times, the happier your outlook on life will become.

CBT Technique #4: Neutralize Negative Thoughts

One way to neutralize negative thoughts is to confront them. Make a list of whatever unpleasant thoughts are burning up your brain waves. Then, systemically go through the list and rate each thought (and its accordant fear) in terms of reality on a scale of one (never going to happen) to five (going to happen for sure). You're looking to train your mind to figure out sooner whether these types of thoughts have any merit or whether they're based on flawed thinking. Ask yourself: "What is the worst thing that can happen here?" or "If this really happens, how will my life be different in a month?"

Another way to neutralize negative thoughts is to challenge absolutes. We all tend to think in absolutes: *If I don't get this done, my boss will fire me.* Or, *If I lose this deal, I'll go broke.* After the fact, when the panic has subsided, you may even laugh about how far you had taken the paranoia. Still, rather than being funny, this kind of black-and-white thinking is unproductive, and you need to break the pattern. The next time you're in one of those situations, take a second to challenge the absolutes your crafty mind is spinning. Nine times out of ten, you've exaggerated the consequences.

Another tactic is to immediately identify and challenge your negative self-talk. These thoughts usually pop up when you're attempting to learn something new and that nagging voice in your mind starts whispering: *You don't know how to ski, you're a klutz* or *You're going to screw up the whole game and make everyone mad.* Again, confront these thoughts directly and flip them by stating more realistic positives: *I've been a klutz in the past, but I'm much more coordinated now and I will master skiing!* Or *It's just a game and everyone is here to have fun—if I screw up, they'll still like me.*

CBT Technique #5: Practice Thought Stopping

Some of us can get so good at negative or obsessive thinking that we produce it without even being consciously aware of it. You may think, "I know I'll make a poor impression at this job interview" the second you set up the interview. This type of negative thinking can happen faster than you can manufacture happy thoughts to counter them. The good news is that you can learn to interrupt these thinking streams and then deal more realistically with them.

One tactic is to interrupt negative thought streams by simply shouting "Stop" to yourself. Then switch to a positive alternative thought before other troubling thoughts emerge. A new thought, such as, "I will be relaxed, positive, and learn a lot from my interview," will allow you to do just that. This is a simple but highly effective technique if practiced regularly.

Debate Yourself

Thoughts of depressed individuals are dominated by negative interpretations of the past, of the future, and of their abilities to overcome setbacks or day-to-day trials. One method to fight negative interpretations of the past is to argue against them. Using an internal (or external) dialogue to combat the logic of pessimistic interpretations has been shown to relieve depression to just about the same extent as does taking antidepressants—with less relapse and less reoccurrence.

CBT Technique #6: Reframe Events

Rarely, if ever, is any event, person, or plan all bad or all good. Tragedies can bring about triumph. We have all heard about or known people who endured catastrophic losses that they then used as a springboard for positive action. People responsible for driving while drunk, who caused a devastating car accident, go on to spearhead drunk driving crusades; people who lost loved ones to cancer go on to create charity drives that bring in millions of dollars for cancer research.

All of us have experienced losses—some of them more extreme than others—but there is often a seed of triumph hidden in them. It may be hard to see at first, but it is there. Try asking yourself: "What is the good in this? What lesson can I take away? How can I share my knowledge with others?"

Bring to mind two or three events that you might have thought to this point to have been totally bad. Write down only the good and/or the benefits gained from each. Even if it takes awhile to come up with a list, positive outcomes are there, lurking under your mound of depressive thoughts. Looking for the brighter side is a great habit to develop. You will be a happier and more compassionate person for it. Interestingly, you can learn to become grateful for life's painful experiences as well as the pleasant ones. It's a tool you can use to choose to live as an optimist as opposed to a pessimist.

CBT Technique #7: Develop Your Ability to Concentrate

We all lead incredibly busy lives, and multitasking has become essential when it comes to coping with all the complex details that fill our lives. Living in this state can overload our brain, with negative thoughts drowning out positive thoughts. One way to combat negative thoughts is to narrow your focus and concentrate on what is going on right now in your life. Unfortunately, the ability to concentrate is becoming a lost art for many, even though concentration is a marvelous tool for retraining your brain to have happy thoughts. If you're having trouble concentrating, try this exercise.

Place a lighted candle on a table about two feet from your chair and concentrate only on the flame. On a blank sheet of paper, make a mark each time you find yourself thinking of something other than the flame itself. Do this for five or ten minutes, per day, for thirty days.

If you practice this religiously for at least a month, you'll notice that your thought diversions lessen substantially over time. And that means you are regaining the ability to concentrate by reducing the volume of unproductive thoughts while attending solely to the object or thought you want to concentrate on.

CBT Technique #8: Create Positive Affirmations

"Some folks think they can. Others think they can't. They're both right."

—Henry Ford

This technique works well for those with low self-esteem or who have developed obsessive or negative thoughts about an upcoming or past situation. Instead of letting a barrage of negative thoughts dominate your life, create a list of positive affirmations to counter them. Suppose you are nervous about going to an out-of-town party where you will know no one except the hostess, who will be very busy. Repeating a positive phrase like, "I will be relaxed, sociable, and have a really fun time" said in five sets of ten each day before the party (fifty times daily) creates a picture in your mind that your brain will be happy to fulfill.

Consider This!

There's always good news out there. Here are some happy results of studies that should cheer you up:

- Seniors who were first told they had an above-average memory performed significantly better on memory tests.
- Seniors who are personally optimistic about their future well-being outnumber those pessimistic about their future three to one.
- The number of people reporting that they were in a "good mood" outnumbered those reporting to be in a "bad mood" twenty to one.
- 70 percent of people met with a smile give a smile in return.

At the very least, formulating positive affirmations will calm your nerves and set the stage for a happier outcome . . . and then you *will* have a great time, which will reinforce positive envisioning for the next event, and the next, and so on. Experiment with positive affirmations in different situations, and then sit back to watch how well your brain functions when it's been instructed to set up the ideal ending.

ENTER MINDFULNESS!

Now that we've covered the basics of CBT, it's time to take another leap forward. Thanks to the groundbreaking research and decades-long devotion of Dr. Jon Kabat-Zinn to mindfulness meditation at the University of Massachusetts, there is abundant evidence that the practice of mindfulness meditation can have astounding effects on your brain's ability to think far more positive thoughts.

It turns out that one of the most effective methods to use your mind to train your brain originated thousands of years ago . . . with Buddhism! Actually, the effects of mindfulness meditation, as practiced by Tibetan monks who still follow the teachings of Buddha (who outlined the principles of mindfulness), are currently being widely researched in the field of neuroscience.

What Is Mindfulness?

Mindfulness is the ability to cultivate awareness of the present moment without relying on our usual, somewhat rote perceptions, thoughts, fears, or judgments. It is being in connection with the direct experience of the current moment, being fully present in the here and now. The practice of mindfulness teaches you how to stay open and learn how to control your own mind, instead of your mind controlling you. One of its basic tenets is to allow thoughts to come and go, without allowing your mind to latch onto one or the other and lapse into your usual obsessive tendencies. Mindfulness trains your mind to direct your attention in a wholesome and healthy manner.

From birth, our minds learn to interpret internal and external events as good or bad, right or wrong, or fair or unfair, etc. Instead of experiencing future events with an open mind, if they are similar to what came before, people tend to react to them in what has become a habitual way of perceiving and responding. In other words, how you felt about the original event affects how you think about, experience, and react to similar events—or events that *feel* similar. Mindfulness allows you to become more aware of your habitual thinking process so you can choose to respond to any situation in an individual way and in a way that's most effective for you—*in the here and now.*

WHAT IS MINDFULNESS-BASED COGNITIVE THERAPY?

Mindfulness-based cognitive therapy (MBCT) marries the practice of mindfulness meditation (see Chapter 5) with cognitive psychology in a way that is distinct from cognitive behavioral therapy (CBT). As you just learned, CBT is about examining your thoughts so you can re-evaluate and redirect thoughts, as appropriate. MBCT employs the tenets of mindfulness meditation (sans any religious aspect) as a way to stay open to the present moment without relying on habitual ways of thinking, feeling, or responding.

MBCT is about engaging your consciousness to notice your thought patterns, as they occur, and diverting or supplanting unproductive thought patterns by focusing on your breath (or your meditation, or a designated object), by being mindful of living in the present moment (as opposed to succumbing to rumination or habitual thought patterns). It's not so much about stopping thought processes as consistently bringing your awareness to what is happening in the present moment. MBCT seeks to defuse negative thought patterns through remaining mindful of what is happening in the here-and-now. Its chief method is mindfulness-based meditation, which we'll discuss in depth in the next chapter.

MBCT Technique #1: Practice a Mini-Meditation

One MBCT method that you can try is to stop whatever you are doing right now, close your eyes, and focus on your breath until your mind quiets. As thoughts arise, allow them to float away by gently redirecting your mind back to your inhalations and exhalations, blotting out whatever is going on around you. Stay in the "mini-meditation" for fifteen minutes, or start with five minutes and work your way up to fifteen minutes. With practice, you can easily learn to quiet any mind chatter that may have been distracting you. It's a great way to refocus when your mind has been wandering.

MBCT Technique #2: Be Fully Present

You can also practice mindfulness by being fully conscious of and engaged in what you choose to do at each moment. For example, if you are chopping carrots for your salad, bring your full attention to the task. Cease all external and internal conversation and focus on the sharpness of the knife blade as it slices into the meaty carrot, the sound of your knife scraping the pieces across the cutting board, the texture and taste of a slice when you pop it into your mouth, and so on. As you will quickly see, mindfulness can be very effective in drowning out distractions and quieting an overactive mind, plus it helps your brain focus on the enjoyment of each experience.

The Benefits of MBCT

MBCT has proven helpful with chronic pain, psoriasis, cancer, health or social anxiety, chronic fatigue syndrome, stress, generalized anxiety disorder, bipolar disorder, disorders involving a history of suicidal ideation or behavior, and even—on a limited basis—with psychosis.

When MBCT Went Mainstream

While Dr. Kabat-Zinn initially focused his work on MBCT on pain management, his success with mindfulness-based stress reduction (MBSR) led three researchers and clinicians (Segal, Williams, and Teasdale) to develop a treatment to address the high relapse rate among those who suffer from depression. According to their research, patients with no history of depression have a 22 percent chance of having another major depressive episode; those with a history of at least three depressive episodes face a 67 percent chance of having another. They theorized that a tendency to suffer depression becomes essentially etched in and used MBCT as a way to help depressives break the mental and emotional pattern that led to relapse, and had astonishing results. Those participants who had experienced three or more episodes of depression cut their relapse rate in half (over the sixty-week follow-up period).

CHANGE YOUR THINKING, CHANGE YOUR LIFE

If you suffer from the blues, have low self-esteem, or tend to expect the worst to happen in almost any situation, you can combat those nagging negative thoughts through a variety of cognitive behavioral therapy (CBT) techniques, such as creating a self-assessment log to bring your thoughts into consciousness, thought stopping, neutralizing negative thoughts, guided imagery, reframing thoughts, and creating positive affirmations.

With repeated practice, over time, you can literally retrain your brain to think happier thoughts and to *expect the best* to happen in almost every situation. You're the one in control, the one who can direct your brain to perceive events and experience feelings and create expectations. Flip off your autopilot switch, and lead your brain down the path to happiness.

One way to flick that switch is through meditation in general, and mindfulness meditation, in particular. Let's learn more about that now.

CHAPTER 5
MEDITATE YOUR WAY TO HAPPINESS

"Thought is cause, experience is effect. If you don't like the effects in your life, you have to change the nature of your thinking."

—Marianne Williamson

Training your mind to be happy through meditation is one of the quickest routes. Studies have shown that directed mental activity can actually affect how your brain works. Studies of Tibetan Buddhists, considered the champions of being happy and the equivalent of Olympian athletes when it comes to practicing mindfulness meditation, revealed that their level of highly focused intention and meditation sharpened awareness and increased empathy, two qualities that play central roles in being happy.

In his book *The Art of Happiness*, the Dalai Lama revealed that his meditation practice embraces the systematic training of the mind to cultivate happiness. He believes that a genuine inner transformation by deliberately selecting and focusing on positive mental states, while also challenging negative mental states, is possible thanks to the very structure and functioning of the brain.

A growing number of neuroscientists are willing to concede that the practice of Buddhism, and mindfulness meditation in particular, may result in changes that have strong correlations with how your mind works. Buddhists believe that you can overcome your past and, through the practice of mindfulness (meditation and living mindfully), achieve enlightenment.

Buddhist principles define a human being as a constantly changing dynamic stream, and in more recent years, neuroscientists have found scientific proof of neuroplasticity, the ability of our brains to continue to grow and form new synapses, which was once thought impossible in adults. Both Buddhists and neuroscientists now view humans as constantly evolving and capable of expanding and improving upon the way our minds think, and thereby the way our brains work.

CREATE INTENTION AND FOCUS

"What is given to the eyes is the intention of the soul."

—Aristotle

In the Buddhist tradition, wise intention is the second step on the eightfold path to the relief of suffering. To Buddhists, emotions and motivation lead to intention and intention precedes action. Nothing happens without intention. All things are first created in the mind and then created in the environment. *Every* thought is truly an intention.

Just Thinking about Compassion Makes You More Compassionate

Researchers working under Richard Davidson at the University of Wisconsin recently measured what happens in the brains of Tibetan monks when they envision themselves performing compassionate acts. They found that merely envisioning their future behavior dramatically increased activity in two areas of the monks' brains: the prefrontal cortex, which flooded them with a sense of well-being, and the areas involved with motor planning, as if they were preparing to leap into action. Dr. Davidson is seeking scientific validation that compassion can be learned, and he suspects that being compassionate toward others may lead to healthy changes in our brains that would then lead to becoming even more compassionate. If this is possible, the Dalai Lama may be proven right after all—he believes that we can change the world through training our brains to be more compassionate.

Your intentions and your *authentic* desires create your world. Your intentions are your high ideals and are usually at the root of your motivation when it comes to reaching for specific goals. Most people don't really want to achieve goals like finding a new relationship, earning more money, or creating a fit body simply for the sake of having those things in and of themselves. They want them because of what they believe they will experience by having a new relationship or more money in their lives. In other words, your authentic, or underlying, desire is likely an intention to be peaceful, grateful, joyous, loving, fulfilled, loved, healthy, or financially secure. By starting with your intentions, you get right to the source of what you truly want. Intentions are the core and the magic of all your goals and desires.

In his book *Love and Will*, psychologist Rollo May noted that the ability to have intentions is the ability to assign meaning to experience, which is essential to living a conscious life. According to May, "Meaning has no meaning apart from intention. Each act of consciousness tends toward something, is a turning of the person toward something, and has within it, no matter how latent, some push toward direction for action."

Therefore, bringing your intentions to consciousness, via meditation or any other method of interior observation and reflection, empowers your consciousness to override any subconscious choices that may be thwarting your efforts to create happiness. Once you bring your intentions to consciousness, you will gain a deepening sense of purpose and clarity. Intentions are very important in your quest for happiness—or for any other goals.

Here's a list of ways that creating intentions benefit your body, soul, and mind:

- They give your brain a sense of purpose and something to focus on.
- They narrow down a field of awareness, which helps your brain regulate and direct its energy.
- They increase self-awareness and perception of what's going on in your mind.
- They disrupt interfering thoughts and reveal a pattern of scattered thinking.

- They help you stay in the now, focused on what you can change.
- They help us define distinction between your inner and outer world.
- They bolster purposeful self-observation.
- They help your unconscious become conscious.
- They let you see and address your resistance.

When Am I Not Myself?

At the University of Pennsylvania, Andrew Newberg utilized imaging techniques to look at the brains of people meditating. He discovered that while meditation caused enhanced blood flow to the frontal cortex and the limbic "emotional" brain system, other areas of the brain showed a reduced blood flow, meaning they were less activated. One such portion of the brain was the posterior/superior parietal lobes, often called the "orientation association area" and can be thought of as housing a three-dimensional picture of the body and where it is in space in relation to other bodies. When this area is quieted in meditation, a person may describe the feeling of self-transcendence—being a part of everything around him or her. Quieting this area can cause a person to place as much emphasis on nonself properties as self properties and increase empathy and understanding.

Your Brain on Intention

Your brain's reticular cortex directs incoming stimulus to your conscious or unconscious mind, serving as a sort of gatekeeper, allowing you to tune in to whatever you decide is important and requires attention. Strengthening this process will help you gain clarity on and consciously create intentions. To fire up your reticular cortex, focus on what you want. Be as specific as you can. Know what you want and why you want it. In narrowing your focus, you will engage your reticular cortex to shut out excess thoughts and distracting sensations, which will help you move beyond wishful thinking and into manifestation of your intentions.

Think of it as developing a superconscious, transcendent mind. Your mind will transcend your everyday concerns and move you into a spiritual mode of thinking (or, perhaps more appropriately, *feeling*). Some would liken it to a religious experience; others to feeling lifted out of their bodies into the realm of superconsciousness.

Keep Your Eyes on the Prize

What happens when your attention on what you are focused on creating becomes interrupted? The dreaded rumination, mindless worrying, fantasizing, or zoning out takes over—harpooning your authentic intention.

When you've identified an intention, focused on it, and made a clear, committed decision to act upon your intention, your developing superconscious, transcendent mind will open the universal floodgates, bringing you all the resources you need, sometimes in seemingly mysterious or impossible ways.

A Consciousness United

If your consciousness is divided against itself, it's practically impossible for your mind to be able to manifest your desires. A wishy-washy intention and a blurry lens doesn't motivate your subconscious to offer up all the energy and creativity you'll need to make it happen. One essential component of learning to use your consciousness to create what you want boils down to this: When you are consistent in your thoughts, your goal will manifest with ease. But when you have wildly inconsistent thoughts about what you want in life, you will encounter conflict and obstacles. To train your brain to work with you on manifesting your intentions, clear the path, sharpen your focus, and get your mental ducks in a row.

MEDITATE ON A REGULAR BASIS

Meditation is a productive way to focus your mind as well as activate your parasympathetic nervous system, the one that lowers your heart rate and slows down your breathing, creating a sense of calmness and stillness. Finding ways to achieve this state of tranquility has been a hallmark of every culture, probably because it fostered a sense of unity and peace. In many cultures, in history and today, prayer has basically served the same purpose, as does hypnosis, guided imagery, biofeedback, and many other modern relaxation therapies.

Basically, for meditation to calm your sympathetic nervous system and activate your parasympathetic nervous system, you need the following ingredients:

- Slow, deep, rhythmic breathing, which slows your heart rate.
- Focused attention on being fully present, which activates your PFC and which calms your amygdala and your sympathetic nervous system.
- A quiet space, which keeps distractions from disrupting your focus within.
- A relaxed posture, which calms your entire body and improves circulation.
- A nonjudgmental attitude, which facilitates objective self-observation of your thought processes and emotions.
- Labeling, which is using words to label any and all emotions or thoughts or fears that arise. This process activates your left frontal lobe, which offers up more positive emotions.

What Type of Meditation Is Right for You?

Meditation helps you cultivate a certain quality of mind by harnessing attention, and focusing and developing concentration. Once you've established a basic comfort level with the process, there are various methods of focusing that you can choose, such as:

- Focusing on breath and body sensations
- Focusing on a visual image
- Focusing on a sound or mantra, such as "om"
- An open-field awareness—focusing without an object in mind
- Focusing on emptiness

Better Than Calamine Lotion

In a 1998 University of Massachusetts study, patients with psoriasis who meditated while receiving ultraviolet treatments for their skin healed four times faster than the control group—regardless of whether they had any previous meditation training. Researchers remain puzzled about exactly how it works, but they have observed that meditation reduces stress and helps people develop a more positive outlook, both of which have been shown to strengthen the body's immune system.

HOW MINDFULNESS MEDITATION CAN CREATE A HAPPIER BRAIN

"You can undergo an emotional re-education. By meditative exertion and other mental exercises, you can actively change your feelings, your attitudes, and your mind-set."

—Francisca Cho, Buddhist scholar

There are, of course, many forms of meditation, but mindfulness meditation, in particular the practices of contemporary Tibetan Buddhists, has been the focus of recent research in relations to neuroplasticity.

In a now famous study at Promega Biotech, Dr. Kabat-Zinn offered an eight-week course on meditation based on Buddhist traditions (although the course was technically nonreligious). Two of his most prominent findings regarding the brain and mindfulness meditation are:

1. Focusing on positive thoughts, while concurrently dismissing discomforting thoughts, reduced stress and increased a sense of well-being.
2. Mindfulness meditation resulted in physical changes in the brain: activity in the prefrontal cortex had shifted clearly toward the left, indicating a strengthening of the associated neuronal circuitry.

As you may remember from Chapter 2, your left prefrontal cortex contains more connections to the emotional centers of your brain than the right prefrontal cortex. Some researchers call the left prefrontal cortex the "emotional" cortex and the right prefrontal cortex the "evaluative" cortex. Thus, strengthening left-centered connections may allow for more control and understanding of emotional responses, and strengthening these connections in a happy or positive state make it easier to reach that state again.

WHY MINDFULNESS MEDITATION WORKS

Mindfulness meditation teaches you how to be more present in the midst of daily life, basically by teaching you how to be more aware of what's going on inside you—your physical sensations, emotions, and thoughts. The ongoing daily practice of mindfulness meditation can help you deal with difficult emotions, such as anxiety and depression, and help you be less reactive and more in the present moment. It's designed to help you learn to find peace within, which will help you weather life's ups and downs, as well as cultivate more compassion, self-acceptance, and kindness, for yourself and others.

Mindfulness meditation involves the following:

1. Paying attention in a particular way
2. Developing the ability to alert and focus your attention

3. Developing the ability to dismiss distractions and direct your thoughts
4. Developing the ability to monitor and redirect your emotions
5. Developing the ability to have a specific goal and exert executive (mind/brain) control to stay on target to get it done

Engaging in mindfulness meditation means you are creating intention and motivation for your mind to alter the way it perceives, receives, and reacts to thoughts and emotions. Practicing mindfulness meditation on a regular basis (once or twice daily is best) brings a sense of equanimity to what is happening moment to moment, training your mind and your brain to observe and embrace (or deflect) anything and everything that traverses its way into your mind—and you are learning to do this without judgment, with acceptance and openness to what is happening in your mind.

Widen Your Perspective

A weakened or underdeveloped ability to focus your attention may be raising your stress level. When your attention is too scattered, it actually makes it easier for your brain to hone in on whatever is causing excess stress in your life, which can lead to a pinpointed negative fixation. Instead, gather your attention and apply it to the task of widening your focus and thereby gaining perspective on the stressful event or situation. Look at all aspects of the event or situation and how insignificant it likely is within the context of your life. This new perspective may, in itself, reduce your stress level. (This exercise would be the flip side of the concentration exercise in the preceding chapter, whose purpose was to help your mind dispense with scattered thoughts and achieve steadier attention on one focal point.)

To Be . . . Is to Be

The goal of mindfulness meditation—whether you're focusing on an image, your breath, or sensations in your body—is to coax your mind into what Kabat-Zinn calls a state of nondoing. This is not the polar opposite of doing, because a lot will be going on during mindfulness meditation, but it will be internal, mind-focused doing. You'll be focusing your mind on the process of releasing thoughts, detaching from emotion, and tuning into what's going on in your body and your mind. The single goal is to learn to be fully present in the present, experiencing each moment as it happens, without judgment, responding emotionally, or issuing a call to action. You are training your mind to simply *be*. And in doing so, you are training your brain to slow down, dismiss distractions, avert negative thoughts, ignore past history, and listen to internal cues.

Float Like a Butterfly

According to Dr. Zindel Segal and Dr. J. Mark Williams, authors of *Mindfulness-Based Cognitive Therapy for Depression*, half of their depressed patients with a history of repeated relapses did not fall back into depression after they used a particular mental technique for observing their thoughts: to regard their thoughts as transient mental events that come and go. In essence, they imagined their thoughts as butterflies.

HOW TO PRACTICE MINDFUL MEDITATION

According to Buddhist master Sakyong Mipham Rinpoche, the easiest way to begin a mindful meditation practice is to meditate twice a day for short periods of time: ten, fifteen, or twenty minutes each. Luckily, you can practice mindfulness meditation in the comfort of your home or anywhere else. It's as simple as creating a physical and mental space that will facilitate the process and allotting at least ten minutes twice a day, at least in the beginning. Later you may want longer, even more focused or guided meditations. Following are the basic guidelines for practicing mindfulness meditation.

Step #1: Create a Space

To calm and center your mind, create a space that will facilitate the process. Even if it's only a quiet nook in your house, having relative peace and quiet will allow you to focus on the meditation with the least amount of distraction. If you have spiritual talismans and their presence lends itself to your practice, by all means have them nearby and integrate them into the quieting of your mind and spirit. Some like to focus on a small talisman that they lay on the floor in front of them.

Step #2: Sit Erectly

Buddhists believe that energy flows best when your body is sitting erectly. You can achieve the desired position by balancing on a somewhat firm pillow with your hips neither thrust forward nor leaning back, and your legs crossed. For those who need to sit on a chair, sitting up straight with your feet flat on the floor will work quite nicely. Place your hands palm upward on your thighs. Some like to touch their index fingers and thumbs together, but whatever feels comfortable and receptive is fine.

Step #3: Inhabit Your Body

Once you are in the correct posture, it's easier to bring your full attention to your body and your mind. Before you meditate, visualize that you have a string running from the base of your spine that you are using to slowly pull each vertebrae upwards into alignment. When you reach your crown, your shoulders and hips should both be level on the pillow or cushion, and you should feel fully present in your body. Ideally, you will feel relaxed but awake. Sleepiness is not the goal, as mindfulness meditation is all about training your mind.

Step #4: Minimize Distractions

If you want to play music during your mindfulness meditation, choose something soothing that relaxes rather than excites your mind. As you progress, you may want to experiment with guided meditations (those led by a taped voice), or you could even create an individualized guided meditation. For strict mindfulness practice, keep your eyes open but softened and facing down, focusing no farther than a couple of inches in front of your nose. This helps you achieve the desired containment of your mind. If you have trouble minimizing your focus, try laying a small object on the ground in front of you and use it to refocus whenever your mind wanders.

Shut Up!

It's fairly typical to have upwards of 300 thoughts in one thirty-minute session of mindfulness meditation—which is why it's so challenging to turn a blind ear to them whizzing past. It's not easy to turn off the thought-generating process, but take heart in knowing that it is possible to do. Labeling your thoughts is one effective method, as long as you label and then release them, of course. Mindfulness meditation is all about staying focused on the now, on simply being. In time, you'll learn how to skillfully allow thoughts to sail in and sail out of the harbor without succumbing to their usual bid to distract you.

Step #5: Breathe

Controlling your breath is also very helpful in slowing your body down and focusing your mind. Begin by focusing solely on your breath, neither forcing nor exaggerating breaths, just noticing as each breath enters and exits your body. As you breathe in and out normally, consciously use the motion of the breaths to relax your body and your mind. If you're a shallow breather who rarely breathes from his or her diaphragm, ease your way into taking slower and deeper breaths. Placing a hand on your bellybutton, so your can feel your belly rise and fall as you breathe in and out, will help you learn to breathe deeper.

Step #6: Unleash Galloping Thoughts

During mindful meditation, the goal is to figure out how to clear your mind of thoughts and focus solely on being fully present and conscious in your body. When your thoughts wander or emotions rise up—and they will, galloping about like wild horses—take notice of where they've gone, label them ("distraction," "fodder for later thought," "the usual fear," etc.), and then bring your mind back to the present, to the meditation. Focusing on your breath is a good way to bring your mind back to the process. While it may feel as if you are wasting time by keeping your mind clear of thoughts, in fact, your mind is learning a new way to slow down, relax, and perceive and process information. You are effectively training your mind to eradicate extraneous distraction and focus clearly on one thought at a time.

Step #7: Cool Down

Once you have meditated for the allotted time, slowly bring your awareness back to the room. A few deep, cleansing breaths is a great way to notify your body and mind that you're transitioning from focused meditation to living in your normal world.

Integrating Mindfulness Meditation Into Your Life

The more you practice mindfulness meditation, the more you will find the process both relaxing and rejuvenating. You may soon also find yourself corralling your mind and living fully present and conscious in your everyday life.

If you're having trouble finding time for twenty-minute sessions, informal meditation practice can be just as important, particularly if you do it ten or fifteen times a day. Knowing how to mindfully meditate first is imperative, but once you do, all you have to do is pause throughout your day (or when you're awake at night) to drop in, taking meaningful pauses to breathe deeply in and out, and focus, however briefly, on being fully present in the moment. If you make dropping in to see how you're doing a habit, it will help you build a mindfulness muscle that will help you stay focused on being in the moment and fully attentive to your intentions and your process.

YOUR BRAIN DURING MINDFUL MEDITATION

Mindful meditation has been shown to be effective in reducing stress, anxiety, and depression, as well as bolstering your immune system. Overall, mindful meditation, practiced on a regular basis, seems to improve coping skills and emotional resiliency. Here's a short list of what's happening in your brain while you mindfully meditate:

- Labeling your emotions with words activates your left PFC, which calms your amygdala and reduces anxiety.
- Engaging your concentration alters the connection between your thinking (cortex) and the emotional (amygdala) parts of your brain, strengthening your neuronal pathways and thus allowing for more voluntary recognition and control of emotions.
- Being fully present activates your cortical networks near your cingulate cortex (increases empathy and self-awareness), the insula (focuses on internal body states), and the somatosensory cortex (senses your body in space), making the focus on *you* and how you are feeling—allowing your own happiness and calm to be the mainstay.
- Engaging in self-observation and awareness activates the middle PFC (center of metacognition, "thinking about thinking" or evaluating one's own reasoning).

Keep Those Brain Pistons Firing

The more brain systems fire synchronously, the better your mental health. Mindful meditation practiced on a regular basis will increase left frontal lobe activity and lower emotional reactivity, as well as help you (and your brain) become more self-observant, positive, and compassion-ate. Mindful meditation tunes up brain circuitry and connects the social circuits of so-called "mirror neurons" that recognize emotional faces in others and help you identify what others feel. It does this by improv-ing self-awareness, cultivating your sense of empathy for yourself, and improving your ability to regulate and consciously express your emotions.

Listen Up, Emotions: *I Am the Boss of You*

Studies at the University of Toronto revealed that people who have completed an eight-week MBSR training are able to activate their insula. Located deep inside your gray matter, the insula informs you of what's happening inside your body in the present moment with-out connecting the experience to a specific emotion. This allows you to break the pattern of responding to new stimuli and experiences automatically. The point of meditation is not to stop you from having an emotional response to what's happening in your life but to avoid responding purely out of habit. Mindfulness reminds you that when it comes to your reactions, you're the one in charge.

LIVING MINDFULLY

Once you've mastered mindfulness meditation, the next step is living mindfully. Granted, trying to live mindfully, fully in the present, in the moment, is not an easy skill to master. It's all too easy to let your daily routines, your habits, and your thoughts swallow your best intentions. Unfortunately, this leaves you feeling disconnected from what is hap-pening around you . . . or even within your own body. Living mindfully involves paying attention to everything that happens within your body and around you in the present moment—without judgment. It means remaining conscious instead of falling sway to your usual patterns of thinking and acting, or, more appropriately, reacting.

A Cousin of the G Spot?

After he performed numerous studies on how meditation affects the brain, Dr. Brick Johnstone, a University of Missouri psychology professor, discovered that, when meditating, a specific change occurs in the right parietal lobe, a region he describes as our "self-awareness spot." According to Dr. Johnstone, meditating decreases the self-awareness spot, which may lead to the *I am at one with everything* feeling that many report during meditation. He also noticed a similar reaction when subjects were engaging in an appreciation of art, nature, and music . . . and when feeling or acting romantic or charitable.

Your brain was designed to categorize and evaluate everything that you think, see, hear, feel, taste, or smell, but unless your mind is consciously piloting your brain, you can veer off course and get lost in all those habitual thoughts. So, work on training your brain to be happier via meditation or mindfulness meditation, and get those neuronal paths cleared for liftoff.

THE MYRIAD BENEFITS OF MEDITATING

Meditation, and particularly mindfulness meditation, has many ways of making you happier, among them:

- **The physiological benefits of meditation:** lowers blood pressure, increases blood flow, reduces headaches, reduces carbon dioxide that causes acidosis and reduction of brain cells, increases serotonin, and decreases cortisol.
- **The mental or spiritual benefits of meditation:** balances your state of mind, increases creativity, increases sense of peace, increases awareness, bolsters positive thinking, elevates your consciousness, and builds confidence and wisdom.

- **The psychological benefits of meditation:** improves empathy and compassion; decreases insomnia, phobias, anxiety, and eating disorders.
- **The brain benefits of meditation:** increases gray matter in the insula, hippocampus, and prefrontal cortex (improves psychological health, attention, compassion, empathy); increases left prefrontal cortex activity (lifts mood); reduces cortical thinning; increases power and reach of gamma waves (more neurons fire together and form new synapses).

By establishing a daily practice of meditation, you are magnifying your chances to be happier, more connected, and better able to solve problems. So grab your favorite pillow, sit yourself down, and breathe in and out. . . .

MEDITATION RESOURCES

You can find more information about the subject of meditation in every medium out there. Here are a few ideas to get you started.

The Mindfulness Awareness Research Center (MARC) at UCLA offers a selection of audio files you can listen to or download. One provides complete meditation instructions, and others offer a variety of length and content options. Once you've familiarized yourself with the technique, you can then opt for mindfulness meditations ranging from three minutes to twelve minutes. There are short and long versions of a breathing meditation, a body and sound meditation, and a loving kindness meditation, among others. Check them out at *http://marc.ucla.edu.*

You can also find a wealth of audio CDs and digital downloads on everything from Qi Gong to Taoist to Kabbalah meditations; Tibetan, Buddhist, Vipassana, and Zen practices; and guided meditations from teachers such as Pema Chödrön, Jack Kornfeld, Thich Nhat Hanh, Jon Kabat-Zinn, and many others on *www.soundstrue.com.*

CHAPTER 6

FEEL YOUR WAY TO HAPPINESS

"Only connect."

—E. M. Forster, from the novel *Howards End*

Some people are just born happy—or are they? Are we born with a genetic level of happiness? One that we have no hope of changing? Perhaps, but the new breakthroughs in neuroscience we've mentioned in previous chapters lead us to believe that neither of those premises is written in stone. We definitely believe that you have the power to move your set point needle closer to the happy end of the spectrum and that you can, indeed, use your mind to *feel* your way to happiness.

First let's take a look at how your own feelings of love, intimacy, security, and support—or lack thereof—are contributing to your happiness right now.

The I Feel Happy Quiz

1. **You believe that:**
   - **A.** Happiness is a state of mind
   - **B.** Some people are born with a capacity for happiness
   - **C.** Some people are doomed by genes to be unhappy
   - **D.** You are doomed by your genes to be unhappy

2. **When it comes to friends:**
   - **A.** You have a wide circle of friends who you see often
   - **B.** You have a best friend who fulfills your need for companionship
   - **C.** You're too busy to hang out with anybody right now
   - **D.** What friends?

3. When it comes to love, you:

A. Are happily married
B. Are a serial monogamist
C. Are lonely but looking
D. Prefer your cat

4. When you screw up, you:

A. Are quick to forgive yourself
B. Forgive yourself eventually
C. Berate yourself for your failure
D. Punish yourself for your failure

5. When you are feeling upset, you:

A. Call your best friend to talk about it
B. Call your best friend but don't talk about it
C. Give yourself twenty-four hours to wallow, then shrug it off
D. Brood by yourself indefinitely

6. You get angry:

A. Infrequently
B. Only when provoked
C. Often, but you control it
D. Often, and cannot control your outbursts

Now tally up your score.

- *If you checked mostly As,* you recognize the impact your feelings have on your state of happiness and work to keep those feelings positive. But there are ways you can enhance those good feelings—and boost your happiness level.
- *If you checked mostly Bs,* you are doing some of the things that generate good feelings that contribute to your sense of well-being, but there are many more ideas you can try.

- *If you checked mostly Cs,* you are allowing feelings of inadequacy, anger, depression, and/or bitterness to diminish your happiness. But you can learn to capitalize on the many opportunities life offers to generate the more positive feelings that can make you happy.
- *If you checked mostly Ds,* you are allowing your feelings to destroy your potential for happiness. But you can break free of the muck of negative emotion and embrace a happier, healthier life.

ARE WE BORN HAPPY?

The presence of an inborn emotionality or behavioral disposition is widely accepted in daily life. For example, even young children can observe that newborns can be somewhat accurately described as happy, quiet, nervous, fussy, etc. That's one reason some scientists theorize that our reptilian brain creates or places us somewhere along the continuum of an emotional tone—creating, essentially, a genetic set point for happiness.

Here's how it plays out in your brain. Nuclei in the reptilian brain may cause some people to have an inborn tendency to live in fear, which would likely cause them to worry unnecessarily and to so strongly imagine danger to be imminent (when it's not) that their brain triggers an overabundant flight-or-fight response. Others might have a more laid-back approach to life, with an emotional range that permits them to remain calm even when confronted with danger (real, not imagined, danger). It may take something truly life-threatening to throw these "cool cats" into the flight-or-fight response, which means their hormonal balances are likely much healthier, if occasionally duller than some would find desirable.

SO WHAT *IS* AN EMOTIONAL SET POINT?

It does seem to be true that each of us has an emotional set point, a *median* that defines our general range of emotions as well as delineates our high points, our low points, and everything in-between. Throughout your day, your different moods, emotions, or feelings travel up and down your emotional scale. Fluctuations occur when experiences affect how intensely you feel, but the median reflects your most predictable emotional self.

Do Opposites Stay Together?

Generally, we are attracted to mates who have a similar emotional set point. If we tend to be happy and content, we attract happy and content; if we tend to be angry and depressed, we attract angry and depressed. Of course, opposites do attract, but it's also true that opposites are perhaps more likely to grow apart, particularly if one effectively shifts his or her emotional set point for one reason or another. More often than not, the other partner will soon feel betrayed, as if he or she "doesn't know who you are anymore" and will rail in arguments that "you've changed."

Someone with a limited emotional range who falls somewhere between feeling angry and feeling crankily discontent, for example, might have a set point that reflects a tendency for worry, doubt, disappointment, and bitterness. This would be their emotional comfort zone, which, would *feel* less than comfortable to other people. But that's *their* accustomed or ingrained emotional set point, how they've learned to react to life.

Narrative Trenches

Though this median emotional set point may exist, we don't believe that it's set in stone at birth. However, we do buy that some people become entrenched in a narrow range of emotions, while others have wild fluctuations, and still others have good moods and bad moods that are balanced and mostly occur in the middle range—between rage on one end and bliss on the opposite. No matter where you live on the emotional scale, most of the time you automatically respond to new experiences based on how you think they will affect you, linking your new thoughts to (conscious and unconscious) past experiences. Your mind/brain assists you in evaluating—in nanoseconds—how you think something is going to make your life better or worse, and then in creating a possible narrative for the experience, upon which *you attach feelings*.

For example, if you are scheduled for an interview and you are delayed in traffic, your mind will likely spring into action, dispensing thoughts and their attentive emotions, such as "Now I'll never get there on time and ruin my chance to make a good impression," or "They'll assume that I'm always late and won't hire me," or "Yippee, now I have a legitimate excuse for not showing up."

Obviously, your interpretation is subjective to your experience, but any of those thoughts will likely have knee-jerk emotions attached: fear and dread if you really want to get to the job interview on time; feeling incompetent and unworthy of trust if this sort of thing always happens to you; or feeling elated and happy if you didn't really want the job and wanted to find a way out.

You Can Rewrite Your Narrative!

Though you may find yourself in your median emotional set point most of the time, it is possible to break out of it if you choose to. Every new situation offers you an opportunity to react in the same old way—or in a new way. Slowing down your reactive response and examining your thoughts—employing tenets of mindfulness, for example—can break your unconscious, automatic response cycle and help you assess and detach in whole new ways. For one, you can realize that stalled traffic, in itself, is neither good nor bad. It is what it is, and nothing more—unless you attach a negative narrative and allow your emotions to go sailing forth uncharted.

The next time you're caught in traffic, try slowing down your brain to match your situation. Rather than allowing your thoughts to career into the negative zone, take in a few slow, deep breaths (remember mindfulness!) and spend a few minutes thinking of positive ways to use your newly freed up time. Perhaps you have a book on CD that you can slip into the player, or maybe it's an album you absolutely love that will cheer you up. See the minutes as a godsend, a time when the pressures of everyday life can subside for a short while, giving your brain time to dream about what you'll have for dinner that night, or where you'll go on your next vacation. Be grateful for the "spare time," and you may find that it passes very quickly and leaves you feeling refreshed.

Chill Out!

According to a study by Ohio State University psychologist Tilmer Engebretson, people who have a trait he called "cynical hostility" (which you might describe as aggressive, angry, or driven) are at greater risk for developing heart-tissue damage than those who have cooler, calmer personalities. A study at Duke University showed that cynicism, mistrust, and aggressive anger increased the death rate from heart disease. If you struggle with feelings of anger, find a therapist, attend a support group, or find some way to focus on positive emotions. Your brain would much rather experience far more soothing emotions.

Your Brain on Narrative Processing

Narrative processing takes place in the medial prefrontal cortex, an area of your brain (behind the center of your forehead) that coordinates complex behaviors and thoughts. Neuroscientists have discovered through neuronal mapping that activity in the right and left prefrontal cortex tends to create a bell curve of variation. Most people's activity falls in the middle, which means their emotions are subject to moderate fluctuations. Those whose prefrontal cortex activity most often occurs farthest to the right are likely prone to clinical depression or anxiety disorders; those whose activity most often occurs farthest to the left rarely suffer from depression and are more likely to bounce back after suffering disappointments.

Your prefrontal cortex is also the site where meandering thoughts originate. Taming those thoughts allows you to loosen your grip on a constricted narrative, and to corral your thoughts so you can focus on achieving your goals.

HOW TO CHANGE YOUR EMOTIONAL SET POINT

Scientists once believed that your emotional set point was fixed at birth. Most based their beliefs on researcher David T. Lykken's study of 1,500 sets of adult twins, 700 of which were identical twins, including sixty-nine identical pairs who grew up in separate homes. When the results were published in 1996, Lykken concluded that well-being and happiness were "at least 50 percent 'inherited.'" Even if that premise held true—and there's new evidence that disputes Lykken's findings—that still leaves 50 percent of your happiness quotient undetermined, i.e., malleable.

Earth to Your Amygdala . . .

If you suffer from mood swings, or often feel as though you have no control over your emotions, learning to monitor and tamp down disturbing emotions will strengthen an array of neurons in your left prefrontal cortex that inhibits—or quiets—your amygdala. Your amygdala is the center of fearful responses, and when it is quiet, you are far less likely to respond to stressful or new situations with a high-pitched emotional response that was designed to deal with life-or-death situations. With enough practice, you can eventually cool down your emotional set point and improve your emotional stability.

As we discussed in Chapters 4 and 5, cognitive behavioral therapy (CBT), mindfulness-based cognitive therapy (MBCT), and other forms of meditation, as well as the practice of living mindfully, can all help you learn to monitor your moods and thoughts, deflecting those that might spin you into the negative zone. Other important elements in creating greater happiness include:

- Getting sufficient sleep and exercise
- Nurturing close relationships
- Maintaining an optimistic outlook
- Discovering and using your best skills in work and play

These techniques are all good ways to strengthen happier neuronal pathways. Now we'll discuss specific things you can do to boost your happiness levels.

ACCENTUATE THE POSITIVE

As we've discussed in previous chapters, increased blood flow and electrical activity in certain parts of your brain can be stimulated by focusing on certain subjects. Tibetan monks, for instance, were able to increase activity in their left prefrontal cortexes by mindfully meditating on compassion and by envisioning acts of compassion.

Read My Face

Dr. Paul Ekman, author of *Emotions Revealed*, studied the facial expression of emotions as telegraphed in rapid, slight changes in facial muscles. These microexpressions, also known as ultrarapid facial actions, cross our faces in as little as one-twentieth of a second. They often unconsciously, and almost always spontaneously and involuntarily, expose what we're really feeling inside. Luckily, the vast majority of people cannot decipher these microexpressions. Dr. Ekman's testing revealed that even those focused on detecting emotions, such as judges, police, and psychotherapists, don't fare any better than the average Joe when it comes to reading these microexpressions. However, when Dr. Ekman tested two Tibetan mindfulness meditation practitioners, one scored perfectly on reading three of six emotions, and his fellow practitioner scored perfectly on four. One American, who taught Buddhist meditation, scored perfectly on all six. Want to understand your love interest or boss or kids better? Time to sign up for mindfulness meditation classes!

According to a report in the 2007 *Journal of Psychiatry & Neuroscience*, there is scientific evidence that self-induced moods, or the thoughts associated with these moods, can positively influence your brain chemistry, specifically benefiting the synthesis of serotonin. In other words, choosing to be cheerful, upbeat, optimistic, hopeful, and happy—even when you *feel* quite the opposite—can create positive changes in your brain chemistry and structure, ones that could turn the tide from glum to optimistic. All the more reason to look on the bright side of life!

TRANSCEND YOUR NEGATIVE GROOVE

People who struggle with feeling blue tend to view their sadness as a problem they need to fix. Unfortunately, when something triggers sadness, they focus on the negative aspects of the situation, which creates a narrow perspective and generates a merry-go-round of nagging questions: "What is wrong with me? Why am I such a loser? Why does everything *always* go wrong for me?" It's like falling into a well of counterproductive thinking.

Ponder This!

Reflective pondering is a casual looking back and reflecting upon what has happened to you in your life. In and of itself, it can be very helpful in reframing events or gaining a wider understanding of why certain things occurred and how you *chose* to react to them, with an eye on how you could choose better or to congratulate ourselves. This kind of reflection can be a positive, growing exercise for your mind—particularly if you forgive yourself and attach some happy thoughts to the memory.

Brooding or negative rumination causes your brain to relive and re-experience negative events as if they are happening all over again—which also triggers the hurtful emotions that were associated with those events. Remember when we discussed your brain's inability to know if an event is really happening or if you're only imagining it? By ruminating, you're *really feeling it* all over again, and again, and again . . . . and again, living in a painful past instead of a more pleasant present. Instead of reliving the traumatic event, either release it or *reimagine it* in the way you would have wanted it to go.

Fertilizers for Happiness

The neurotransmitters serotonin and dopamine not only play a central role in creating the chemical reactions that lead to *feeling* happy, joyful, upbeat, optimistic, etc., they also play a key role in sowing the seeds of happiness. Serotonin and dopamine help your brain grow new dendrites, which leads to the strengthening of synapses and growth of new synapses. Higher serotonin levels, in particular, keep your gray cells alive and multiplying (depression has the opposite effect). If you want to be happier, find activities that stimulate the production and circulation of serotonin and dopamine in your brain. Those would be activities that bring you *pleasure*, or make you feel good about yourself, others, and life.

Excessive rumination eventually fogs your brain and leaves you brooding about problems that no longer exist anywhere—except in your mind. Brainwise, you are reinforcing negative connotations and interpretations associated with that memory, strengthening the synapses attached to negativity and despair, and taking brain space away from more positive emotions. This increases the probability that every time you think of what created these spiraling thoughts you will feel sad. And that is the *exact opposite* of where you want to be, which is why we're here to help train your brain to be happy!

BECOME THE ANTI-RUMINATOR

If you're a ruminator, try taking concrete steps to break free of your negative groove and focus on creating a positive groove, one that allows you to see the brighter side of everyday situations, to be more emotionally resilient and more adaptable in your relationships. Here's a list of actions you can take to get off the merry-go-round of negative rumination:

1. **Fact-check with friends** to see if your thinking or assumptions are distorted, or if you're placing way too much emphasis on what occurred. Don't assume; fact-check!
2. **Think about something else.** As we discussed in Chapter 4, deflecting or distracting thoughts can be very effective. Remember that meditation techniques such as seeing thoughts as butterflies help negative thoughts flit in and out of your consciousness. Remember, it's *you* who attaches emotional weight to them.
3. **Forgive yourself for whatever you construed that you did wrong.** It's highly likely that you're being too judgmental and treating yourself harshly. We're all human and we all make mistakes. Learn from your mistakes, but don't belabor them. Treat yourself the way you'd treat someone you love.
4. **Release hurtful events that you cannot change.** If it's something you can change, make restitution and patch up misunderstandings; if it's something you can't change, move on.
5. **Brainstorm solutions instead.** Break the circle of negative thoughts by focusing on positive solutions. Enlist your creative brain—your prefrontal cortex and your cerebellum—in coming up with a list of things you could do next time. Your brain is a great resource; use it to its best advantage!

6. **Talk it out.** Ask a friend or loved one to help you sort it out. If that's too painful, call a friend and exchange the conversation in your head for a cheerful conversation about movies or books—something off-topic and uplifting.
7. **Do something fun!** Studies have clearly shown that *doing* something breaks obsessive thoughts. Doing something fun will get you off the beaten track so you can more easily turn off the scratched, broken record of rumination.

I'm in a Happy State of Mind

According to Robert Holden, PhD, author of *Happiness Now!*, the first and most important step to achieving happiness is intention: *deciding* to be happy. In other words, you make it your *intention* to be happy each day. "'Intention' is another word for 'focus,'" Holden explained. "Whatever you focus on will become more apparent and will grow. For centuries, optimists and pessimists have argued over who's right, and the answer is they both are; each sees what they're looking for. If you focus on happiness, that's what you become more aware of."

VALUE YOUR FRIENDSHIPS!

According to happiness research, friendship has a much bigger effect on average on happiness than a typical (average) person's income. Companionship stimulates your brain's attachment and social group circuitry, which helps you feel both safe and loved. According to a survey out of the National Opinion Research Center, on average, the more friends you have, the happier you are. Furthermore, friendship itself lights up your brain in all the right areas. In October 2010, researchers at Harvard University found that brain areas associated with calm, familiarity, and happiness—particularly the medial prefrontal cortex—would respond more strongly when people were thinking about a friend versus a stranger with similar interests (such as a work colleague). This activation persisted even if the friend had a dissimilar lifestyle. So if you can't see your friends, at least think about them often.

Why You Never Have to Feel Alone Again

When friends and family are unavailable, remembering how you felt on your last social outing with them essentially tricks your brain into re-experiencing the same positive, loving feelings you typically feel when they *are* around. Drs. Hansen and Mendius, writing on the issue of compassion, report that simply recalling being with someone who really loves you—re-experiencing the feeling of giving and receiving loving care—activates the deep attachment circuitry in your brain. In other words, your brain doesn't care if the objects of your affection are near or far, only that thinking about them fires up the neuronal connectivity associated with feeling loved.

Social closeness makes your brain happy. If you're feeling lonely or sad, get out in the world and make new friends—your brain will love you for it. Social isolation, whether real or imagined, is very bad for your brain. Regular connection with other human beings maintains healthy neurons. A study published in 2008 showed that socializing and mental exercises have very similar effects in terms of improving brain functions. More than 3,600 people were tested in this study, which showed that, even at the age of ninety-six, more socially engaged people did just as well (or better than) others in the same age group on tests of cognitive function, even after controlling for physical health and daily activity levels. Stay connected and your neurons will stay healthy!

FALL IN LOVE

Among the findings of many subjective well-being studies is that we have a critical necessity for close connection, physical touch, and the deeper embrace of love. Nature armed our brains with potent neurotransmitters that will draw us to others—as long as we show up and do our part.

Through the Looking Glass

Sometimes a mirror can be an excellent friend. Our mirror neurons play an important role in our quest for love. Mirror neurons are active when someone else performs an action or makes a facial expression, and you then perform the same action or make the same facial expression. It's like the neural correlate of recognition and empathy. Intimacy that involves emotional connectivity, empathetic recognition, active listening, and feeling mutual love fires up your brain's mirror neurons, which react as though *you yourself* were feeling happy or sad, or acting depressed or hurt. This deep social recognition smoothes the way for increased compassion and improved relationships in all areas of your life.

Love Potion Number . . .

In the beginning stages of romance, endorphins—our body's natural morphine—are released when we feel pleasure, excitement, and love. Endorphins and the hormone vasopressin, which has been shown to be critical in pair bonding, flood the brain and play a role in attracting suitors. Endorphins, of course, simply feel good, leaving those besotted by a mutual attraction desiring more frequent contact and a deepening connection in order to feel good over and over again. The ups and downs of early romance often intensify the release of dopamine, which fuels the attraction, but as the relationship solidifies, oxytocin plays a more central role in cementing the bond. The hormone oxytocin is well known for its role in mother-child bonding during pregnancy and lactation, but it also serves as the "love hormone" because it stimulates long-term pair bonding, orgasm, and social recognition.

Basically, your brain loves intimacy, particularly when you are fully present and interrelating—and the longer and deeper your love, the more your brain responds. Keeping excitement alive will throw a little dopamine in the mix, so be spontaneous, creative, and attentive to your love!

If You Want to Be Happy . . . Get Married?

The desire and need for emotional connection are often the foundation for happiness, and having these needs fulfilled through love and marriage apparently makes a whole lot of people happy. Studies have consistently found that married people are happier than unmarried people, even as much as *twice as happy* as unmarried people. In a National Opinion Research Center survey of 23,000 Americans, conducted over the last two decades, 41 percent of married people described themselves as "very happy," while only 22 percent of those who had never married, or who were divorced, separated, or widowed, chose that description.

The Couple That Meditates Together Stays Together

In recent research, Virginia Tech's Marriage and Family Therapy Program discovered that meditation might be another tool for increasing empathy in relationships. In their study, high-conflict couples that started meditating (by focusing on one word or a phrase for ten minutes at a time, together or alone) soon reported that they argued less often. Other studies have also found that when couples meditate together, it may only take a few weeks before both partners experience increased sensitivity to each other's feelings.

Of course, it's difficult to determine if these results occur because happy people tend to get married or if being married leads to greater happiness. A 2003 study reported in the *Journal of Personality and Social Psychology* revealed that happy individuals appear more likely to get married—and stay married. Psychologist David Myers found that the benefits of marriage—intimacy, commitment, and support—are largely responsible for his subjects' emotional well-being and most likely outweigh whatever unhappiness might result from the usual stresses that occur within marriage.

Being *happily* married (or mated outside the legal definition of marriage) has another benefit: According to research, married men live seven years longer than those who do not marry, and married women live four years longer than unmarried women.

FOCUS ON GRATITUDE

"Reflect on your present blessings, on which every man has many, not on your past misfortunes, of which all men have some."

—Charles Dickens

Experiencing gratefulness has many benefits, one of which is improving the way your brain works. Studies have shown that people who compiled a list of things they were grateful for—each day, for thirty days—changed the way their brains work. Dr. Daniel G. Amen has taken brain images of healthy individuals before and after concentrating on feelings of gratitude for several weeks. He found that after contemplating on gratitude, some limbic areas of the brain (such as the thalamus and the medial prefrontal cortex) were very active, while limbic areas associated with negative emotions (such as the amygdala) were quieted.

Even better news: It doesn't matter if events or memories you call upon to feel gratitude are twenty years old or happened on the day you write the list. It's the mental act of *re-experiencing* pleasant memories and *feeling* grateful that evokes positive emotions and increases your ability to live in the moment, and to feel compassion.

So many things can engender gratitude, even if they're small—like sharing a pot of tea with a friend, walking through the woods at sunrise, reading the latest spy thriller, taking your dog to the beach, watching your child play in a pile of leaves, loving the way your new haircut makes your hair swing while your walk, having 400-thread-count sheets, and so on. The important thing is to make a list every day for thirty days, until feeling grateful becomes a habit.

Your Brain on Gratitude

When you focus on what you love about your life, your positive emotional brain fires up. Areas like your thalamus and hypothalamus, which are important in processing positive emotions associated with love, sex, and companionship, are active, while *negative* areas, especially the amygdala, are quieted by your prefrontal cortex. All of this makes for a focused, positive, emotional feeling free of worry and fear, allowing you to truly enjoy moments of happiness.

Before you go to sleep each night, write down at least five things you're grateful for and pause to re-experience the pleasure each brings you. Focus on what is making you feel lucky and good about your life, and you will soon find that you feel more positive in general and that you begin to slow down to savor the good times. Your brain will love you for this, and so will those around you.

PRACTICE FORGIVENESS

"The practice of forgiveness [is] strongly linked to happiness."

—Christopher Peterson, PhD, University of Michigan psychologist

Forgiveness leaves your factual memory intact but removes and even transforms the emotional sting, making it an effective way to diminish painful synapses so you can create more pleasurable synapses. Forgiveness is not an erasure of the past; it is a marvelous way to change the emotional projections that a memory carries (because *you* attached deep meaning to what happened when it occurred).

Forgiveness reduces the energy necessary to maintain your anger towards someone who has offended and hurt you. It's good for body and soul:

- Forgiveness helps your body because it lowers blood pressure and reduces the risk of ulcers and even cancer.
- Forgiveness helps your soul because it allows your happiness to reach newer and higher levels.

Here are a few suggestions to help you forgive:

1. **Record and release.** Write down every detail you can possibly remember about the offending event and/or the offender. Get it all down in black and white . . . *but don't share it with anyone!* This process is designed to facilitate release, not to sustain arguments. Burning it is a great way to watch all your painful thoughts go up in smoke.

2. **Identify, empathize, and altruistically forgive.** Make a list of the possible thoughts and feelings that you imagine motivated him (or her) to do what he (or she) did. Identifying reminds you that we're all human and we all make mistakes. Empathizing will soften your heart—both toward the person who hurt you and toward yourself. If you're human, you've also wounded someone. Imagine how good it would feel to be resolved of your wrongs, and then extend that same kindness towards your offender.

3. **Commit to your decision to forgive.** If necessary, write a declaration of forgiveness or a sacred promise to live in forgiveness in regards to the event. Again, please don't show it to the offender, who likely is not in the same emotional space as you are. Besides, this process is about how *you* release the negativity connected to the event and to the person. Store your promise or certificate in a drawer and pull it out whenever memories resurface—and they will.

Forgiveness is about empathy and altruism and love . . . but it's also about releasing negative emotions so they aren't gumming up *your* emotional synapses. Employing empathy and altruism is a great way to complete the process and bolster happier synapses. It's about releasing the negative so you can focus on the positive, so that both the offender and you can move on. If it doesn't get the job done the first time around, repeat the steps until you have truly erased the pain associated with the event(s) and forgiven the person who offended you.

And don't forget that forgiving *yourself* is also important to the process!

ENERGIZE YOUR EMPATHY

Empathy is your ability to feel someone else's pain—or joy. Scientists believe that the ability to feel empathy is hard-wired, but it's also similar to a muscle that needs to be flexed. If you're not happy in your life—or if your most basic needs are not being met—it's harder to feel empathy. Also, if your family or culture didn't model empathy, the neuronal connections required to identify deeply and compassionately with another may not be sufficiently developed.

One of the best ways to develop empathy is to seek out opportunities to offer love, acceptance, understanding, and compassion. It's all about *feeling* emotionally attached to someone, *feeling* sympathetic to her situation, or *feeling* genuinely happy for his success. It's all about love!

It's as simple as this: Giving *feels* good. Effort spent identifying what another really can benefit from, in a lasting way, stirs feelings of empathy and love. But giving without knowing the other person can be even more rewarding. Giving anonymously—and spontaneously—can *feel* extremely gratifying. This manner of giving means not expecting something in return—the true meaning of altruism. Giving from your heart connects you with mankind, expands and fulfills that *you* in you (which some call your soul), *and* it boosts serotonin levels.

Spread That Serotonin Around

When you do something kind for someone else, you're not the only one whose serotonin levels rise. The person you're helping also has serotonin released in her brain—she feels happier, even if she doesn't know why.

Remember that giving doesn't have to be about money or possessions. Give someone your place in the grocery line; give someone a muffin in the morning; write someone a cheerful message; tell someone you love him or her—and why. In other words, share your glad tidings.

IF ALL ELSE FAILS . . .

Being prone to negative rumination often leads to depression, but you can train your brain to think—*and thereby feel*—more positively. Clinical trials have shown that using mindfulness-based cognitive therapy (MBCT) is more effective than antidepressants at reducing the rate of depression relapse. It works because it teaches participants to break negative thought patterns. Typically, the classes offer a blend of mindfulness-based meditation with therapy. You can find MBCT programs by logging onto *www.MBCT.com*.

But we have another idea, as well. If you're having trouble thinking, meditating, or feeling your way to happiness, it's time to revert to what worked when you were a joyful child. It's time to *play* your way to happiness.

CHAPTER 7

PLAY YOUR WAY TO HAPPINESS

"The abilities to make new patterns, find the unusual among the common, and spark curiosity and alert observation are all fostered by being in a state of play."

—Stuart Brown, MD

There's a reason kids look so happy. It's because they're allowed—even encouraged—to play. When it comes to happiness, we have a lot to learn from kids. Play can lay the groundwork for a healthier, happier brain. And not just because it's fun but because it stimulates your mind and keeps your brain supple.

How play-full is your brain?

The Play Happy Quiz

1. **You do thirty minutes or more of exercise:**
   - **A.** Five days a week
   - **B.** Three times a week
   - **C.** Twice a month
   - **D.** Never

2. **You think of exercise as:**
   - **A.** Fun
   - **B.** Critical to your health
   - **C.** A necessary evil
   - **D.** Little as possible

3. You have sex:
A. At least three times a week
B. Once a week
C. Once a month
D. You can't remember the last time you had sex

4. You take a vacation:
A. Every weekend is a vacation!
B. Twice a year
C. Once a year
D. What's a vacation?

5. You love a good game of:
A. Geocaching
B. Bridge
C. Solitaire
D. You never play games

6. When I want to learn something new, I:
A. Celebrate my progress with rewards
B. List my goals and check them off as I achieve them
C. Quit halfway through the process
D. Wait until the feeling passes.

Now tally up your score.

- *If you checked mostly As,* you have made play a part of your lifestyle, but you can still allow yourself to play harder—just like a kid and as happily.
- *If you checked mostly Bs,* you occasionally indulge yourself in play, but you need to make more time in your life for fun, to give your brain the recess time it needs to bolster your physical and emotional well-being.
- *If you checked mostly Cs,* you have forgotten how good it feels to play. You are undoubtedly bored, stressed out, and/or lethargic. You

need to get out and have some fun, for your body and your brain's sake.

- *If you checked mostly Ds,* you are missing out on life's greatest pleasures. All work and no play is dulling your life—and destroying your potential for happiness.

WHY PLAYING IS ESSENTIAL TO HAPPINESS

Playing (or exercise or stimulating mental exercise) stimulates your brain's pleasure centers. Basically, playful activity stimulates your basal ganglia (coordination of movement and feeling) and your deep limbic system (emotional intensity, passion), and the combined stimulation alerts your prefrontal cortex (thinking) that this is fun! To maximize enjoyment and reinforce the good feelings, your ventral tegmental area starts pumping out that neurotransmitter that we love so much: dopamine. Your hypothalamus gets in on the act as well, secreting oxytocin, vasopressin, and endorphins.

The upshot is that your brain goes on a holiday, a delicious, nutritious, and hopefully vigorous holiday. Obviously, the more pleasurable experiences you create, the happier you'll be—as long as you don't succumb to addictions or excessive irresponsibility.

We're all for playing your way to happiness, so let's begin with playful activities that also involve exercise!

CHOOSE PLAYFUL EXERCISE THAT WILL MAKE YOU FEEL HAPPY

According to author David Rakel, author of *Integrative Medicine*, more than 10,000 trials have examined the relationship between exercise and mood, proving beyond a shadow of a doubt that physical exercise is a mood lifter. In some cases, exercise has proven just as effective as psychotherapy in treating clinical depression. We all know exercise is extremely good for our overall health and well-being, but here are a few superlative reasons why exercising (particularly aerobic exercise) is a great way to train your brain to get happy:

- Exercise stimulates circulation and increases blood flow to all parts of your body and brain, bringing extra oxygen, glucose, and nutrients. The extra blood flow to your brain provides the perfect environment for creating and strengthening your little gray cells. Exercise keeps your brain well nourished, youthful, receptive, flexible, and finely tuned.

- Exercise that involves coordination between your muscles and your brain activates your cerebellum, which improves your ability to think and helps you think faster and think better!

- Exercise increases self-esteem and confidence, which makes you more able to engage with others (remember how important friendship is?) and enjoy life. It just makes you feel better about yourself, and that's worth its weight in gold.

- In addition, exercise helps increase healthy growth factors in the memory center of your brain—your hippocampus. Researchers at the University of California–Irvine have also demonstrated that the changes that take place in your brain as a result of exercise—increased neurogenesis and rejuvenation and generation of neural connections—occur because exercise stimulates certain types of genes known as neural growth factors. These neural growth factors contribute to strengthening your memory. With consistent, moderate exercise, you'll retain the ability to recall happy memories longer and more often.

It Just Gets Better with Age

The effects of exercise on your brain never cease; in fact, as you get older, exercise becomes even *better* for your overall brain health. Neuroscientists have shown that in aging populations (usually those over age sixty-five), sustained, moderate exercise participation enhances learning and memory, improves the function of the neocortex (especially the PFC), counteracts age-related and disease-related mental decline, and protects against age-related atrophy in brain areas crucial for thinking and learning. Exercise has been cited by

several researchers, including those at the University of California–
Irvine, as being the *number one factor* in sustaining brain health and
the ability to make new neurons in an aging brain.

Do What You Love

Best of all, it doesn't even matter what kind of exercise you choose
(although aerobic exercise that gets your heart pumping is best). You can
jog five miles or walk around your block; mountain climb or swim at
your local gym; go deep-sea diving or plant a garden in your backyard;
lift weights in a gym or ride a bicycle in your local park; go bowling in a
dive or play tennis at the country club; go kayaking or take boxing lessons; take intensive yoga classes or practice tai chi. As long as you move
your body regularly, it will boost your happiness levels. But if you pick
something you love doing, you'll be stimulating your pleasure centers at
the same time.

Exercise Your Brain, Too!

Numerous studies have shown that people who lead lives with little
mental stimulation experience greater cognitive loss as they age.
Their memory fails with greater frequency, and they find it increas-
ingly difficult to work puzzles, perform mathematic equations, and
do other mental feats that come quite easily to people who exercise
their brains often. Maintaining mental acuity is like training to be a
professional athlete; you need to do something every day that revs
up your brain and flexes your gray matter. Treat your brain like a
muscle, one that needs a strenuous workout on a regular basis.

The U.S. federal guidelines for exercise say that getting at least thirty
minutes a day most days a week will help prevent heart disease, osteopo-
rosis, diabetes, obesity, and, perhaps, Alzheimer's disease. Brisk walking
for thirty minutes a day is all that is needed for brain health—and it

doesn't have to be thirty consecutive minutes. You can walk briskly for ten minutes three times a day, or for five minutes six times a day.

REWARD YOUR BRAIN FOR NEW ACTIVITIES

If you have a problem motivating yourself to exercise, we have the perfect solution—trick your mind to fall in love with exercise. Even if you harbor a thousand negative connotations to exercise and (like most of us) have failure etched into every memory associated with exercising, we have an ingenious, brain-specific solution: reward your brain instead!

Pair Up the Activity with Pleasure

For instance, let's say you're starting a new exercise routine, something you've attempted and failed to achieve many times before. To create new neuronal pathways that will support rather than diminish your will to succeed, consciously use your mind to pair up the new activity with something you consider rewarding. It could be stopping for a cup of tea with friends on the way home from yoga class, buying your favorite magazine after working out at the gym, or calling your new girlfriend after a round of tennis. Whatever you choose, make it something that brings a *genuine* feeling of pleasure to you, and keep it up! Do it the second, third, and fourth time you exercise as well.

Importantly, the reward should take place during, or *immediately after*, the activity. Rewarding yourself will link the new activity with positive associations and good consequences, thus reinforcing new, more positive brain connections. Soon you'll be thinking of this particular form of exercise as something you love to do, and you won't need that original reward anymore in order to feel just as good.

Reverse the Process to Break Bad Habits

Likewise, if you want to train your brain to abandon negative habits, either teach your brain to consider these habits neutral (avoid linking the negative behavior or thoughts with rewards or punishments) or teach your brain to associate them with bad circumstances (punishments).

For example, instead of getting yourself worked up over the fact that you smoke one cigarette a day, remove all thought from the act of smoking that one cigarette. Don't attach negative or positive action, thought, or emotion. Neutralize it. Remember how effective it was when you actually managed to ignore your two-year-old when he threw a tantrum in the supermarket aisle?

Extinction: Not Just for Dinosaurs

Neuroscientists call the process of extinguishing behavior *extinction*. It can sometimes be a difficult process, but it always eventually works. Back to the example of the two-year-old wailing in the grocery store: The first time you ignore the tantrum, the child might scream louder and longer. These are the cries of the brain cells, which are used to getting a reward for the screaming (recognition, a treat, a hug, or even the simple attention of yelling) and now are getting nothing for the same behavior. The same thing happens with most other habits—at first, you will have a strong drive to continue doing whatever was rewarding before, because it's easy and your brain is used to it. Getting through that part of extinction—the initial meteor strike!—is the hardest part. It gets easier and easier after that, however, and soon you won't even remember what was rewarding about the habit in the first place!

Or, if that doesn't work for you, try following up the act of smoking that cigarette with something unpleasant, such as scrubbing your toilet, paying bills, or listening to heavy metal music at a ridiculously high volume. Whatever it is, it should be something that you genuinely *dislike*, and you should force yourself to do it *every time* you have that cigarette (or enlist someone else to help with the punishment, such as a spouse, child, or close friend, if you can't bring yourself to do it). Soon enough, the cigarette will probably not seem worth the hassle, and you will abandon the habit.

The more your mind controls your emotions and thoughts in regard to undesirable habits, the more your brain will diminish the neuronal connections that led you down the same old path. Associating certain kinds of thoughts with no meaning, no reward, and no punishment will eventually extinguish those thoughts.

Respect Your Elders . . . Elder Brain Cells, That Is

Cells in the lining of our mouth and intestines live for only a few days, and red blood cells live an average of three months. But nerve cells—which generate while you're still floating in your mother's uterus—can live 100 years or longer! It was once thought that nerve cells weren't replaced when they died, but recent studies show that new nerve cells can arise in a few regions of the brain, even in older brains. So it's very important to continue to stimulate your brain, not only to improve the longevity of your existing nerve cells, but also for production of new nerve cells. Your brain and body do their jobs by ensuring an ongoing process of cellular detoxification and repair, but it's up to you to provide the nurturance and stimulation required to keep your brain cells awake and alive.

STIMULATE YOUR BRAIN BY GIVING IT NEW EXPERIENCES

As we've discussed throughout this book, introducing your brain to new experiences helps it form new neuronal pathways. And the more you do something, the more synapses your brain fires and creates. Novelty is great because it will stimulate synapses that have lain dormant or create entirely new ones, because your brain is trying to adapt to process and understand whatever it is that *you* deem important.

If you're athletic, try something that will flex your cerebellum more than your biceps, like learning to play the piano or the oboe. If you're an obsessive reader, try learning table tennis (which is supposed to be one of the best physical activities for your brain because it involves anticipation, memory, analysis, and physical coordination, all at a very rapid pace). If you haven't read a book in five years, try writing an essay on something that taxes your brain (like the latest developments in neuroscience and how they affect your ability to learn a new language). If you never go more than thirty miles from home and rely on the same tried-and-true routes, plan a 100-mile trip, mapping out back roads that will lead you somewhere exciting (using GPS is cheating!).

Better Late . . .

When studies were conducted that asked healthy seventy- and eighty-year-olds to perform the same complex tasks of memory, attention, and learning as young adults, the seniors performed worse, but only if they were under a time constraint. When given enough time, they achieved the same scores as the young adults. The takeaway: When you're learning something new, be patient with yourself and the process. Your gray matter still has the juice, it just flows a tad slower.

Like exercising, it doesn't matter *what* you do as long as you do something that will engage and challenge your brain. Picking something you find intriguing or joyful will strengthen your resolve to keep doing it—but you won't know how much you like it until you try it. We'll get your started by listing activities known to be good stimulators for brain growth, but once you get the hang of it, make up a list of things you would enjoy that would spice up your life and challenge your brain—and then get busy!

Novel Ideas for Stimulating Your Brain

Activities that will stimulate brain activity include:

- **Learn to read music and play a musical instrument.** Reading music and playing an instrument has consistently been shown to morph your brain in ways that few other activities can. Even listening to music has been shown to enhance your "creative process." If you're already a musician, take up sculpting or fly-fishing. You get the drift . . . challenge your mind and your coordination by doing something you've never done before, something that makes you—and your brain—grow.

- **Learn to speak a foreign language.** Join a club that requires you to only speak in the new language—good for your brain and fun! Learning a new language is challenging, but learning to speak in the new language fires up sections of your brain that may have been lying dormant for decades.
- **Trace your family's genealogy** and compile enough stories to write a long "historical tale" about your family's history. If you don't have—or can't find—all the facts, make up detailed stories for your grandchildren that would be close to the truth. The point is to strive to do something that requires mental focus, repetitive learning, and persistence.
- **Learn how to play complicated card games.** There's a reason little old ladies love to play bridge, and it's a good reason—it keeps their memories sharp, and it allows plenty of time for hanging out with people whose company they enjoy. Even gossiping requires and stimulates memory retention.
- **Play trivia games,** or—better yet—make up your own trivia games. The older you are, the more likely it is that you'll forget the answers by the time you summon friends or family to play. Or have each player make up trivia . . . you get the idea. Be creative and exercise your memory!

Live It Up!

If you find yourself pining for the happiness of your childhood, stop and instead enjoy the present. Relying on the results obtained from three large samples of adults studied over several decades, psychiatrist George Vaillant observed that the contributions of mature defenses against despair—such as altruism, sublimation, suppression, humor, and anticipation—play a significant role in living a successful and joyful life. So much for the good old days of your youth—the *really* good days are right now!

STIMULATE YOUR PLEASURE CENTERS

Since negative thinking can deflate your spirits and lead your brain down the ruinous path to depression, it only makes sense that doing things that bring you pleasure and joy can boost your spirits, lead to happy thoughts, and benefit your brain. And playing is all about having fun and boosting optimism.

Why Everyone Needs Stress Busters

Chronic stress kills . . . *literally.* It's been widely shown to have disastrous physical effects, but did you know that chronic stress also diverts energy from your brain (fogs up your mind), shrinks your hippocampus (slows memory and learning), compromises neurotransmitters (limiting joy *and* plasticity), and even emits toxins that attack your brain? Forget zombies; stress eats your brain! Make it a priority to relax. Doing things that are physically and mentally stimulating and energizing is fine, but they also have to be relaxing—with an emphasis on fun!

Pleasure and Enjoyment: Two Peas of the Same Pod?

Before you leap into joyful play, do you know the difference between pleasurable and enjoyable? Pleasure is the yummy feeling that comes from satisfying homeostatic needs, such as hunger, sex, and bodily comfort. Enjoyment, on the other hand, derives from the good feelings you experience when you break through the limits of homeostasis and into the realm of the thinking mind—when you accomplish something that stretches your limits or breaks new ground, such as exceeding your own and others' expectations (such as, in an athletic event, artistic performance, or academically), performing a good deed, or participating in a stimulating conversation. Pleasure for pleasure's sake serves a purpose and is fabulous, but you also want to find enjoyment that will lead to personal growth and long-term happiness.

Ready, Set, Have Fun!

Though it may seem silly to spend time planning something fun, if you are overtaxed or chronically stressed, you may need to do just that. To begin, make a list of ten activities that bring you pleasure and ten activities that bring you enjoyment. In case you need greater clarification, here are two lists to spur your creative process. The first is a list of suggestions for activities that might bring you pleasure, and the second is a list of suggestions for activities that might bring enjoyment.

Things that might immediately stimulate your pleasure centers:
- A romantic dinner date in your favorite restaurant
- Soaking in a tub filled with luxurious bath salts
- A hot stone massage at your favorite spa
- A long walk through the woods
- Taking your dogs to the beach
- Sitting by the fire while reading a great novel
- Trying out a new recipe
- Buying new sheets in your favorite color
- Romping under the sheets with your significant other

Things that might bring enjoyment (*and* stimulate your brain's quest for new experiences and learning new tasks):
- Learning how to create your own website
- Practicing the piano
- Going somewhere exotic that you've never seen
- Planning and planting a garden in your backyard
- Taking flying lessons

- Putting together a 1,000-piece puzzle
- Teaching your daughter to knit
- Going to yoga classes twice a week
- Learning how to ballroom dance
- Taking a photography class

Create your own lists, using your brain to come up with ideas that are both creative and surprising. Flex that imagination, fire up those brain cells, let your inner child explore, and have fun with the process and the execution. Challenge yourself to come up with fresh ideas each month and open up your mind to suggestions.

As you enjoy new experiences and conquer challenges, take time to fully savor each moment. Then, on the days you're not feeling the *go-out-there-and-do-it* vibe, you can call up those memories—in detail—and give your brain the same thrilling experience all over again.

Your Brain Likes Anticipation

Anticipation is often sweeter than the actual experience, particularly when the upcoming event is guaranteed to be pleasurable, such as going out on a romantic date or taking a beach vacation. Anticipating future rewards lights up the pleasure centers in your limbic system, especially your nucleus accumbens, in the same way experiencing the event does. Think about it: You feel butterflies and grin endlessly an hour before that hot date. This is because your brain recognizes all of the situations leading up to the ultimate reward. So dream up something that will lead to joyful anticipation. Even if making it happen seems an impossibility, envision what you'd like to happen, in minute detail, savoring each mental picture. Remember that visualizing something intensely can trick your brain into thinking it's an actual experience. So it really is almost like being there.

HANG OUT WITH FRIENDS AND FAMILY

As the song (sort of) goes . . . *people do need people.* Humans were not designed to live alone, and there's a plethora of research to prove that living isolated from others, or not receiving love and attention, can lead to a host of mental and emotional problems. From the moment we are born, we not only need someone to take care of us physically, we also crave affection and attention, so much so even the simple stimulation of touch plays a role in whether or not we blossom into healthy happy children and adults.

Once again, nature created our brains to know that we need other people. Your brain responds by releasing internal opiates—endorphins— that create that lovely feeling we experience when near someone we love and trust. Studies have consistently shown that feeling close, connected, loved, and supported improves your health and overall sense of well-being. Some studies have reported a lowered incidence of anxiety, depression, suicide, illnesses, high blood pressure, heart disease, and even cancer.

Harkening back to what we learned about the brain, fostering close relationships stimulates your PFC, orbital frontal cortex (OFC), your anterior cingulate, and mirror neurons—yes, those little neurons that allow us to identify with and grow closer to other humans. Some scientists refer to this area as your social brain. Flexing your social brain stimulates your pleasurable limbic system while quieting your fearful amygdala. In other words, it helps you tamp down anxiety and more deeply feel love, connection, support, encouragement, and so on.

HAVE MORE SEX

One of the best parts about being married or in a long-term relationship is that you get to have sex on a regular basis. (Or at least that's a reasonable supposition for those whose marriages and relationships tend to last!) Why? Because sex creates a host of feel-good hormonal and chemical reactions that tend to strengthen the emotional bonds of matrimony

. . . or lustful long-term relationships. You might think of sex as being something that primarily makes your body feel good, but it's oh-so-good for your brain, too!

Your Brain During Sex

It doesn't take a neuroscientist to figure out that sex makes us happy. For most of us, having sex creates pleasurable feelings that (we hope) lead to orgasm. Many areas of your brain are involved in creating and processing the pleasure from sex, but there are three big ones:

1. When engaging in flirting, foreplay, and the ultimate act itself, your ventral tegmental area (VTA) is spilling out dopamine at a mile a minute, most of which makes its way to the limbic area called the nucleus accumbens. This nucleus is at the seat of both seeking and enjoying pleasure; it's active when you're *pursuing* the act of sex and also enjoying the fruits of your labor.
2. That big boost of dopamine in the accumbens is what makes you feel great, and it makes you crave more and more sensation.
3. The dopamine from your VTA also causes signals to go to your PFC so that you understand *why* and *how* you're getting to have all this great fun!

An orgasm provides the biggest blast of legal, naturally occurring dopamine available to your brain. Dutch researchers, after scanning the brains of lucky volunteers experiencing orgasm, likened their brain scans to scans of people experiencing heroin rushes! Not only do you get that huge rush of stimulating neurotransmitters, but orgasm may also release a rush of oxytocin (also known as the "love hormone"), especially in women. Oxytocin cements a strong social connection bond with the person closest to you when orgasm was achieved. Dopamine provides the rush of attraction, but it is oxytocin that will make you associate that pleasure with a particular someone. It also brings that sense of euphoric calm after orgasm and is key in relieving stress, which, as you now know, is a brain killer.

How Sex Benefits Your Brain

In case you've been going through a long, dry spell, here are five great reasons to keep sex on your brain:

1. The more sex you have, the more vasopressin and especially oxytocin you produce. Both of these neurotransmitters strengthen a long-term relationship by linking the physical closeness of your partner to feelings of trust, empathy, and generosity. It's why sex is so important in marriage and why sexless marriages tend to fall apart at some point.

2. Oxytocin also works as a neuromodulator and can sensitize your body's response to endorphins, which often act as natural painkillers, particularly for headaches. Yes, that's right, having sex can *cure* headaches.

3. Sex increases blood circulation, which pumps oxygen to your brain—and to your skin—creating the highly desirable postcoital glow.

4. The more sex you have on a regular basis, the more your blood circulation improves, which helps keep your body healthy and functioning overall, and keeps you—and your brain—youthful. Sex is great exercise! If you're not in the mood, take a minute to envision how good it will feel to have oxytocin and dopamine lubricating, nourishing, and regenerating your neurons. That should get you going.

5. In addition, having sex boosts your natural collagen production, which minimizes age spots and sagging. We don't know of anyone who wouldn't be happier if his or her natural collagen kept pumping up his muscles or keeping her skin youthful.

Also, having an orgasm has been shown to decrease chronic pain by 50 percent, and having sex three times a week has been shown to decrease the chance of heart attack and stroke by 50 percent, especially in women. And, having an orgasm can be a religious experience—or at least as close to one as some may get. Researchers in Finland stumbled on this juicy bit of information while researching blood flow and activity patterns in the brain. Rather inadvertently, they discovered that a religious experience and having an orgasm both light up the outside of the right temporal lobe—what some scientists refer to as your "god area." Hallelujah!

Why Novelty Keeps a Marriage Alive

When you are first attracted to someone, your dopamine levels catapult your brain into the stratosphere. That's why love at first sight occurs and why courtships are usually intense and filled with passionate encounters, all of which is nature's way of making sure you mate. However, the first rush of excitement fades and so does the release of excessive amounts of dopamine. To revive the level of dopamine needed to feel madly passionate, you will need to add novelty. And, no, a new partner is not required. Use your imagination (which is also great for your brain) and come up with a list of novel ways to romance your partner. Choose one a week—just for fun—and watch what happens.

FIND SOMETHING TO LAUGH ABOUT

Laughing is the cure for whatever ails you. Laughing has amazing benefits, including:

- It beats back the tide of stress hormones (cortisol, in particular), giving your body a healthy break.
- It lowers blood pressure and reduces the risk of blood clots.
- It strengthens your immune system.
- It generates the release of endorphins.

In the 1980s, author Norman Cousins documented his firsthand experience of "laughing himself well" in a book entitled *Anatomy of an Illness*. After unsuccessfully enduring a round of medication designed to combat a debilitating immune disorder, Cousins decided to fight it with laughter—and high doses of vitamin C. He spent months watching funny movies or television shows, and discovered that laughing heartily decreased his pain and permitted restful sleep. Over time, his condition vastly improved, leading him to tout that laughter was, indeed, the best medicine.

Get Your Smile On!

Studies have shown that a baby smiles 400 times a day, children up to preschool age laugh about 300 times a day, and adults laugh an average of fifteen times a day. Research has shown that the act of smiling can lighten your mood. If you're feeling down, take a walk around your office and smile at your coworkers. Before long someone will tell a funny story, and you'll all feel better.

Don't underestimate the magic of laughter. Watch movies or shows that make you laugh. Better yet, combine social activities with laughter, such as going to a comedy club with friends, playing board games with your children, doing something silly that makes you and your companions look and feel ridiculous, pulling a string around your house and taking delight in your cat's predatory leaps to snag it. Do whatever it takes to lighten up and put a genuine smile on your face.

LEARN THE ART OF SAVORING

This idea may seem obvious, but in reality, our lives are so jam-packed with activity that slowing down to savor the fun times—the delicious tastes, the enticing smells, the stunningly beautiful sights, and the good feelings they generate—rarely happens. If this sounds all too familiar, you need to learn the art of savoring.

Choose a pleasurable experience each day and slow it down. Let's say you're taking a walk. Along the way, stop in your tracks and slowly take in a panoramic view of your surroundings. Pause to smell a flower or pet your neighbor's dog. Stop occasionally to slowly breathe in the fresh air and feel it replenishing your lungs. Allow the smell of the season to revive memories of happy days in your past. Or spend a half hour truly listening to Mozart, lingering in a fragrant bath, or massaging your lover's hands. The point is to luxuriate in whatever sensual activity brings you physical, mental, and/or emotional pleasure.

Go Forth and Spend . . . ?

Yes, even in an economic downturn, spending money can make you happy—as long as you spend money *doing things*—and not on *stuff*. Spend your hard-earned cash on pleasurable or enlightening *experiences* like concerts, vacations, trips to art museums, lectures on neuroscience (or poetry or whatever fascinates you), cooking classes, a yoga workshop, or a night out with friends. Participating in experiences has been shown to provide more long-lasting happiness than buying things. Plus, research has shown that giving to friends and strangers decreases stress and contributes to enhanced mental health. Spending money on other people, such as family and friends, is a great way to boost your happiness levels—and to get out there and have fun with those you love.

To savor, eliminate distractions so you can bring your full attention to the activity. Turn off the TV, cell phone, and Internet. Focus on noticing and enjoying each and every physical sensation: the sights, sounds, tastes, aromas, and so on. Recognize every aspect that feels pleasurable and *slowly* drink it all in. Notice how your body feels when you succumb to the pleasure it brings, and add an auditory component—humming or whispering sweet nothings will add to the experience.

Enjoying these pleasant life experiences in depth allows you to "smell the roses" and train your brain to more fully experience a higher level of zest and happiness. The more you practice this habit, the more positive your overall outlook on life becomes. *Enjoy!*

Set Your Joy Alarm!

When James Baraz, a founding teacher of Spirit Rock Meditation Center in California, created a class entitled Awakening Joy, the class filled up rapidly. Baraz's idea was to help students "lead their minds toward states of happiness and well-being" by offering a ten-month series of exercises, lectures, and meditations focused on joy. Each activity was designed to facilitate the understanding that happiness is more about having a healthy mental attitude toward whatever you're experiencing.

Here are some elements of Baraz's Awakening Joy class that you could adopt:

- Be fully present for whatever you're doing.
- Define joy, making the meaning specific to what brings you joy.
- Create a list of activities that make you happy, update it regularly, and use it as a checklist.
- Practice some form of physical movement (yoga, dance, walking, etc.) a few times a week.
- Find and check in with someone who shares your quest for joy. Make him or her your joy buddy.
- Sing happy songs every day—even if you sing off key.
- Notice what it *feels* like to be fully present in your body when you're happy.

TIRED FROM ALL THAT FUN?

We hope this chapter inspired you to make room for having a lot more pleasurable fun in your life, not only to cheer you up, but to also stimulate and keep your brain young. After all that playing, you must be tired! Next we'll discuss the importance of sleep, which is another activity that plays a crucial role in brain health and happiness.

CHAPTER 8

SLEEP YOUR WAY TO HAPPINESS

"Sleep is the golden chain that ties health and our bodies together."

—Thomas Dekker

You can eat right, you can exercise regularly, and you can stimulate those little gray cells, but if you don't get enough sleep, happiness may still elude you. Why? Because sleep is one of the most significant indicators of well-being. Sleep well and you live well. Happiness, as it turns out, is often a matter of Zzzzs.

Let's begin by evaluating the quality and quantity of the rest you receive each night—the rest that's so critical to your mental, emotional, and physical health.

The Happy Sleep Quiz

1. Each night you sleep an average of:
   A. Seven and a half hours or more
   B. Six to seven hours
   C. Four to six hours
   D. Sleep? Who needs sleep?

2. You take a thirty-minute nap:
   A. Every day
   B. Three or four days a week
   C. Saturday and/or Sunday afternoons
   D. Naps? Those are for kids

3. **Every night in preparation for bed, you:**
   A. Crawl under the covers and are asleep within minutes
   B. Read in bed until you fall asleep, usually within the hour
   C. Fall asleep watching TV on the couch
   D. Lie awake for hours trying to fall asleep

4. **You're usually asleep by:**
   A. 9 P.M.
   B. Midnight
   C. 2 A.M.
   D. Dawn

5. **You think of a good night's sleep as:**
   A. Critical to your health and well-being
   B. Something you know you need but don't get
   C. A necessary evil
   D. An impossible dream

6. **When you dream, you:**
   A. Write them down in your dream journal upon awakening
   B. Forget them, unfortunately—you think they were cool!
   C. Have nightmares and wake up screaming
   D. You never dream

7. **You suffer from:**
   A. No sleep disorders
   B. Restless legs syndrome
   C. Chronic insomnia
   D. Sleep apnea and/or narcolepsy

8. **When the alarm rings in the morning, you:**
   A. Turn it off and roll out of bed, raring to go
   B. Turn it off and lie there until you're more fully awake

C. Hit the snooze button and go back to sleep—more than once

D. Sleep through the alarm because you were up half the night

Now tally up your score.

- *If you checked mostly As,* you understand the importance of sleep and strive to get enough of it. But there are still ways you can better harness the power of sleep to increase your happiness.
- *If you checked mostly Bs,* you get almost enough sleep to function at your peak, but never quite enough. Reviewing your sleep habits will allow you to improve your sleep patterns, giving your brain the rest it needs to bolster your physical and emotional well-being.
- *If you checked mostly Cs,* you are sleep deprived, along with 40 percent of the American public. Such sleep deprivation adversely affects your health and happiness, often in ways you're not even aware of.
- *If you checked mostly Ds,* you number among the 70 million Americans who suffer from sleep disorders—sabotaging virtually every aspect of your waking life.

Sleeping Beauties

If you want to know how happy a woman is, ask her how much sleep she gets. If it's not much, odds are she's not very happy. A recent *Science* journal study tracked the moods of nearly 1,000 women as they went about their daily lives—and revealed that the top two predictors of unhappiness were stress and lack of sleep.

WHY SLEEP IS SO IMPORTANT TO YOUR HAPPINESS

Sleep is your body's time to restore, renew, and reorganize itself—from head to toe. While you sleep, your cells mend, your energy replenishes, your mood stabilizes, your brain repairs, and your health optimizes. To realize the most benefit, you need to sleep 7½ to 9 hours each night. This allows your body to alleviate the damage caused by stress, ultraviolet rays, and other harmful environmental exposures.

60,000 Reasons to Sleep Late

An extra hour of sleep per day—the equivalent of a nice long nap—will give you a "happiness boost" comparable to a $60,000 annual raise, according to the Franklin Institute.

Also, your cells produce more protein while you're sleeping than when you're awake—and you need these protein molecules to help your other cells repair and recharge. In addition, adequate sleep allows all of your body systems to regroup and reboot, which boosts your energy level upon awakening and helps carry you through your day.

WHY YOUR BODY NEEDS SLEEP

"Metabolic and endocrine changes resulting from a significant sleep debt mimic many of the hallmarks of aging. We suspect that chronic sleep loss may not only hasten the onset but could also increase the severity of age-related ailments such as diabetes, hypertension, obesity, and memory loss."

—Dr. Van Cauter, University of Chicago

A good night's sleep gives your entire system a boost. Here are four more reasons to make sure you get your beauty sleep each night:

1. **Sleep is good for your heart.** If you get fewer than seven and a half hours a night, you run the risk of high blood pressure and cholesterol, both of which sabotage your heart health. This may be why heart attacks and strokes occur more often in the early morning hours.

2. **Sleep reduces stress.** As we've seen, stress is one of the leading predictors of unhappiness. Lack of sleep compounds the adverse effects of stress. When you don't get enough sleep, your body basically goes into high-alert mode, which causes your blood pressure and your stress hormones to spike. The longer you go without enough sleep, the worse this state of hyperarousal grows, according to researchers at Pennsylvania State University's College of Medicine. If you suffer from chronic insomnia, then you are effectually in a state of sustained hyperarousal of the body's stress response system. Not a happy state of affairs.

3. **Sleep keeps you young!** Lack of sleep increases stress hormones and the level of inflammation in your body. Excess inflammation increases your risk for heart disease, cancer, diabetes, and—you guessed it—premature aging.

4. **Sleep helps you lose weight.** According to recent research, people who sleep fewer than seven hours each night are more likely to be overweight or obese. The hormones ghrelin and leptin, important players in regulating appetite, are disrupted by lack of sleep.

The Senior Sleep Advantage

A good night's sleep even helps you live longer. In a groundbreaking survey of the elderly in China, the nation with the world's largest senior population, researchers found that people aged 100 and over slept better than their younger sixty-five- to seventy-nine-year-old counterparts. The study, which appeared in the *Sleep* journal, also revealed that the worse the sleep quality, the worse the health problems—regardless of age.

THE PHYSIOLOGICAL AND EMOTIONAL HAZARDS OF TOO LITTLE SLEEP

"The ideal amount of sleep is closer to 8½ to 9 hours . . . an hour less a night consistently is enough to start to see impairment in people's cognition and mood. Delayed reaction times, glucose load, depression, headaches, and hormone balances can be negatively affected after one night of sleeping six hours or less."

—Dr. Lisa Shives, medical director,
Chicago's Northshore Sleep Medicine

If you think that not getting enough sleep now and then doesn't affect you, think again. Most sleeping experts agree that sleep deprivation can have immediate consequences. If you're not getting your seven and a half to nine hours of sleep a night, you may experience such symptoms as:

- Fatigue, lethargy, and lack of motivation
- Moodiness and irritability
- Increased risk of headaches, particularly migraines
- Reduced creativity and problem-solving skills
- Inability to cope with stress
- Reduced immunity; frequent colds and infections
- Concentration and memory problems
- Weight gain
- Impaired motor skills and increased risk of accidents
- Difficulty making decisions
- Increased risk of diabetes, heart disease, and other health problems

In short, a sleep-deprived you is a sluggish, cranky, forgetful, indecisive, ineffective, inefficient, stressed-out you—*not* a happy you. On the other hand, a well-rested you is an energetic, cheerful, creative, capable, cooperative, energetic, mellow you—a *happy* you.

WHY YOUR *BRAIN* NEEDS SLEEP

It's not just your body that needs sleep; it's your brain as well. Sleep is essential to your healthy brain functioning, affecting genetic processes, protein synthesis, and myelin formation. (Neurons require myelin to transmit messages quickly over long distances.) In fact, recent discoveries have revealed that sleep allows new neurons to grow in your hippocampus, the part of the brain that regulates long-term memory and spatial navigation. Adequate restful sleep also improves your brain's ability to focus, learn new skills, and remember important information.

Sleepy = Hungry

Go without enough sleep for only a week, and your skinny jeans may not fit any more. Sleep deprivation makes you hungrier—as the level of ghrelin, the hormone that regulates your appetite, rises, and the level of leptin, the hormone that curbs your appetite, drops. You'll crave starchy, high-carbohydrate foods, sweets, and other high-calorie foods. This hormonal imbalance can seduce you into consuming as much as 33 to 45 percent more high-calorie foods than your well-rested peers.

What Happens When Your Brain Doesn't Get Enough Sleep

Lack of adequate, restful sleep can have immediate and devastating effects for your brain. Although it's highly unlikely that you'll literally go crazy if you don't get enough sleep, it is worth noting that sleeping problems occur in almost all people with mental disorders, including those with depression and schizophrenia.

Extreme sleep deprivation can lead to a seemingly psychotic state of paranoia and hallucinations even in otherwise healthy people. Disrupted sleep can trigger episodes of mania, agitation, and hyperactivity. What constitutes severe sleep deprivation? Not sleeping for three or four days, or sleeping erratically over an extended period of time.

Sleep Deprivation Really Is Torture

Hallucinations, increased sensitivity to pain, and susceptibility to brainwashing (which can occur after as little as forty-eight hours without sleep) make sleep deprivation a favorite interrogation tool. In fact, sleep deprivation is consistently named by the U.S. State Department as torture in its annual human rights abuses reports.

Even moderate sleep deprivation may slow down your brain, prevent neurons from regenerating and firing properly, limit the formation of new synapses, prevent the plasticity that allows your brain to learn new tasks, and impair memory.

Sleep Your Brain Supple

Deep sleep promotes brain plasticity. Researchers at the University of California–San Francisco studied the effects of deep sleep on brain connections in kittens, after the kittens experienced an environmental challenge. The animals that were allowed to sleep for six hours after the stimulation developed *twice* the amount of plasticity compared to kittens kept awake afterward. The finding has broader implications for plasticity in the brains of adult animals—and humans.

HOW MUCH SLEEP IS ENOUGH?

While most of us won't go more than one night without at least *some* sleep, far too many of us don't get an optimum amount of sleep each night. According to the National Institutes of Health, the average adult sleeps fewer than seven hours per night. Given that we're supposed to get seven and a half to nine hours of sleep a night, this means we are a nation of sleep-deprived citizens.

If you're a working parent, a full seven hours of sleep a night might sound ideal—if only you could manage it. But even that is not enough.

Sleep Less, Die Earlier

In a 2010 study published in *Sleep*, researchers from the University of Warwick, England, found an association between early death and short sleep duration. While they haven't completely proven cause and effect, they did find that the link is stronger for people, especially men, who have sleep apnea, but early death has also been linked to men who sleep less in general.

While sleep requirements vary slightly from person to person, most healthy adults need this seven and a half to nine hours per night to function at their best. Why? Because this is the time your body needs to downshift into dreamland, where your brain goes into overdrive.

New Moms Need Uninterrupted Sleep

The reason new mothers are sleep deprived is not the quantity of sleep they get, as they average just over seven hours per night. It's the quality, reports a new study in the *American Journal of Obstetrics and Gynecology*. Their sleep is interrupted, keeping them up an average of two hours in the middle of the night—and thereby disrupting their sleep cycles. This leads to significant daytime fatigue. The solution? Have Dad handle one of the nighttime feedings (using pumped breast milk or formula) so Mom can sleep. The old adage to "sleep when the baby sleeps" is also a good rule for daytime—provided the nap lasts at least two hours.

Dreamland: Where Quantity *and* Quality Count

Quality sleep allows plenty of time for you to experience the full progression of several sleep cycles—a progression that constitutes a good night's sleep. Each cycle encompasses the five levels of sleep: two phases of light sleep, two stages of deepening restorative sleep (slow-wave), and rapid eye movement (REM) or dreaming sleep.

HOW SLEEP WORKS: THE FIVE STAGES OF SLEEP

When you fall asleep, you cycle through these five stages every 90 to 110 minutes, with the deep restorative sleep and REM sleep playing the most crucial roles. These stages are:

- **Stage 1: Transition to sleep,** which lasts about five minutes. Eye movement slows down, along with muscle activity.
- **Stage 2: Light sleep,** which lasts ten to twenty-five minutes. This stage is characterized by slower brain waves punctuated by infrequent surges of accelerated brain waves.
- **Stages 3 and 4: Deep, restorative (slow-wave) sleep,** which shortens as the night progresses. The deepest stage of sleep, this slow-wave sleep features extremely slow brain waves. During this phase, blood flow is directed away from the brain and toward the muscles, and the synthesis of protein increases.
- **Stage 5: REM sleep** first occurs seventy to ninety minutes after falling asleep. This is the dreaming phase, when the focus is on brain restoration. Eyes move rapidly, breathing is shallow, arms and legs are temporarily "paralyzed," and heart rate and blood pressure increase. Increased protein production occurs. The length of time spent in REM becomes longer as the night progresses.

In the beginning of the night, you spend more time in deep/deep restorative (slow-wave) sleep and less time in REM sleep; however, as the hours pass, you shift out of deep restorative (slow-wave) sleep and into having more REM sleep. (Slow-wave sleep prepares your brain for REM sleep.) In the hours before waking, you're spending almost all of your time in stages 1, 2, and REM sleep, with only brief passes into deep, restorative sleep.

Happiness Is a Sleeping Baby

Babies spend nearly 50 percent of their sleep time in REM sleep. In contrast, adults spend only 20 percent of their sleep time in REM sleep—and that percentage drops as we age.

Your Body on Slow-Wave Sleep

During the slow-wave or deep restorative phase, the focus is on your body, which gets busy conducting all the restorative work that keeps it functioning optimally. Slow-wave sleep also paves the way for REM-stage sleep to replenish and renew your brain.

Your Brain on REM Sleep

During the REM phase, the focus is on your brain. Your breathing grows shallow, your muscle activity slows, and your heart and blood pressure increase, all of which helps your brain take center stage. During REM sleep, your brain:

1. Consolidates and processes any and all information you've learned during the day.
2. Forms neural connections that strengthen and consolidate memories.
3. Replenishes its supply of neurotransmitters, including chemicals such as serotonin and dopamine. These chemicals help all parts of the brain to stay on track—neither too fast nor too slow—allowing the brain as a whole to hum along, doing the best job it can.

Sleeping also increases brain connectivity or plasticity, which helps you continue learning and growing as you age.

BUILDING HAPPY MEMORIES

Getting enough slow-wave and REM sleep is the key to processing memories. And a good memory is one of the hallmarks of happiness. The better your memory, the more likely you are to be a "glass is half-full" kind of person.

People with good memories also tend to be more confident, hopeful, adaptable, and content than those with poor memories, according to a recent study by the University of Stirling in Scotland. They also enjoy more successful relationships and careers. People with poor memories are more apt to obsess about their problems and dwell on disappointments.

REM sleep is when you consolidate your memories, but for REM to work properly, all sleep stages must occur. Especially important is the sequence of slow-wave to REM sleep. Skip slow-wave sleep, and memory and learning suffer—even when REM sleep occurs.

The Tag Team of Memory

Slow-wave sleep and REM sleep work hand in hand, according to a study done at the University of Massachusetts. In the study, people were asked to remember a list of word pairs (a very common memory task). Those who slept before the test did better. More important, those who had more slow-wave sleep *and* REM sleep did the best of all.

THE REM OF LEARNING

Learning and memory are intricately connected—making REM sleep critical to both. A Rockefeller University study involving rats illustrates how certain brain cells activated while we're awake tend to reactivate during REM sleep—helping us remember what we've learned during the day.

In this experiment, researchers exposed one group of rats to novel, enriched environments (labyrinths with toys) and limited another group of rats solely to their cages. During slow-wave sleep (body restorative sleep), the gene zif-268, which is critical for the plasticity of neurons *turned off* (deactivated) in all the rats, regardless of which environment they had experienced. But during REM sleep, zif-268 *turned on* in the cerebral cortex and hippocampus of the labyrinth rats but did not reactivate in the caged rats. The scientists concluded "this retrieval of zif-268 activity during REM sleep may work in consort with other reactivated brain mechanisms to process memories of novel experiences."

Learning Boosts Happiness

Learning a new skill boosts your happiness level—even when the process is challenging. According to a recent San Francisco State University study, people who master a competency—from mathematics to driving a car—experience increased feelings of happiness and satisfaction, no matter how hard-won that mastery may have proven.

Other studies by the same group showed activation of the amygdala (a region of the brain very important in emotional processing) in the same way the cerebral cortex was activated. Scientists speculate that when an experience triggers an emotion, such as fear or happiness, the amygdala may be activated during sleep as a means of processing or reinforcing the emotional connection, just as other parts of your forebrain process the more technical parts of the new experience.

DREAM ON

"Dreams are the mechanism whereby the brain incorporates memories, solves problems and deals with emotions. In this way, dreams are essential for our emotional health."

—Rosalind Cartwright, PhD, Professor and Chairman, Department of Psychology, Rush University Medical Center, Chicago

You typically spend more than two hours each night dreaming. In the REM phase, the pons, located at the base of your brain, sends signals to the thalamus, which relays them to the cortex, the outer layer of the brain that is responsible for learning, thinking, and organizing information. (Remember, the cortex is the part of the brain that interprets and organizes environmental information during consciousness.) Scientists believe that the cortex tries to interpret the random signals it receives from the pons and the thalamus, essentially creating a story out of fragmented brain activity.

Falling into a deep sleep fosters dreaming; dreams help your brain process what has happened throughout the day. While your body slumbers, via dreams, your brain makes connections between events, sensory input, feelings, and memories. These memory links are essential to healthy brain functioning, which improves your waking memory.

The Happy Consequences of Lucid Dreaming

Lucid dreaming is when you know that you're dreaming—whether you come to realize that during the course of a regular dream or go straight from wakefulness to dreaming (known as WILD, for wake-initiated lucid dream). Knowing that you're dreaming allows you to control your dreams, and their effects on you, according to studies by Stanford University and the Lucidity Institute. You can use lucid dreams to boost your self-confidence, enhance your imagination, overcome grief, practice creative visualization (particularly in the area of healing), and reduce nightmares.

The best way to induce a lucid dream? Get about five hours of sleep, then wake up and concentrate on what you want to dream about for an hour. Then drop back off to sleep, and dream your way to a happier waking life. It's important to note that you should only interrupt your sleep when you know you'll be able to sleep for another 2½ hours, and that you refrain from any stimulating activity during your wakefulness period.

GET THE SLEEP YOU NEED TO GET HAPPY

As we've now seen, fostering deep restoration (slow-wave) sleep and REM (dreaming) sleep are both crucial to your brain's ability to process, retain, and assimilate what occurs during your waking hours. Getting enough sleep and helping your brain achieve the deeper sleep levels is highly advantageous to your overall health and happiness. Here is what to do and what *not* to do to improve your overall sleep quality.

What Not to Do
Don't Exercise Two Hours Before Bedtime
Exercising tends to stimulate cortical alertness, which is not a good thing when you want a good night's sleep. Exercise can help decrease stress, but strenuous aerobic exercise puts the nervous system in a state of moderate arousal, which is ideal for mental tasks but not for sleep. Try not to exercise within two hours of your bedtime, and if you must do strenuous exercise in the evening, try consuming a light snack containing carbohydrates and dairy products just before bedtime.

Don't Drink Alcohol an Hour Before Bedtime—and Don't Drink Excessively
Alcohol consumption reduces the relative amount of time spent in REM sleep. The more alcohol you consume, the less REM sleep you get and the less rested you feel in the morning. If you drink alcohol in the

evening, leave at least one hour for the alcohol to metabolize. Also, alcohol is dehydrating, so make your chaser a tall glass of water.

Don't Overload Your Stomach

Eating a large meal in the evening sends your digestive system into overdrive, which will interfere with sleep, especially the deeper phases of sleep that are so crucial to your body and your brain. Also, avoid fatty and spicy foods, as both can disrupt sleep. In general, don't eat a heavy meal within four hours of your bedtime.

Don't Smoke Before Bedtime

Smoking in general is not good for your body in any way, shape, or form. When it comes to sleep, heavy smoking in particular can disrupt REM sleep, cause a person to linger in lighter stages of sleep, and cause awakening in the middle of the night due to nicotine withdrawal. Yet another good reason to do whatever it takes to stop smoking!

What to Do

Stick to a Regular Bedtime Schedule

Try to get out of bed at the same time each morning, even if it's a weekend or holiday.

Create an Ideal Sleep Environment

Moderate the temperature to somewhere between 68°F and 72°F. Close any curtains that can effectively block sunlight or streetlights. Limit noise and distraction, such as television.

Wind Down after a Long Day

Meditation; relaxation exercises; slow stretches that involve slow, rhythmic breathing; and writing in a journal—are all sleep-oriented activities. Tackling a complex work project, watching a violent movie, or reading crime thrillers: not so good. Choose activities that give your mind a rest.

Create a Bedtime Ritual

Just as we use storytelling and lullabies to help our children sleep, we can benefit from a regular nighttime ritual. Climbing into bed with your favorite (lighthearted) novel and a small cup of chamomile tea might do the trick. Whatever you choose, make it something that helps you relax and do it for ten minutes every night.

Limit Caffeine

All types of caffeine affect your ability to fall asleep and stay asleep. Coffee is the most well-known offender, but caffeine can also be found in tea, cola, chocolate, and decaffeinated coffee. Other sources of hidden caffeine are pain pills, weight-loss pills, diuretics, and cold medicine, all of which may have enough caffeine to equal one cup of coffee.

Your Brain on Sleep Drugs

One in four Americans relies on sleep-inducing drugs to get a good night's sleep, according to the National Sleep Foundation. The trouble is, even over-the-counter sleep medications—as well as any medication with the tag "PM"—may increase your risk of cognitive impairment. According to a study by the University of Indiana, this risk worsens with age, to the point of causing delirium in people over the age of sixty-five.

Try Drinking Milk

Milk products stimulate melatonin production, which improves sleep. Whether skim or fat, milk, like complex carbohydrates, contains L-tryptophan, the amino acid that is a precursor of melatonin and serotonin.

Have a Light Snack

Eating a light snack may help you fall asleep. Simple sugars and fats reduce the oxygen supply to the brain, which decreases alertness and makes you sleepy. Foods that contain L-tryptophan include bananas, oats, and poultry. Yogurt and crackers or a piece of bread with a small slice of cheese are perfect bedtime snacks.

Use Natural Sweeteners

If you drink a hot beverage, sweeten it with honey, sugar, or other natural flavoring. Food additives in general and artificial sweeteners in particular tend to increase alertness, and thus interfere with sleep. As a bonus, honey contains the sleep-inducing L-tryptophan.

WHEN TO CALL YOUR DOCTOR

Sleep problems, including snoring, sleep apnea (excessive daytime sleepiness), narcolepsy (excessive daytime sleepiness that can cause unintentional sleep, termed "sleep attacks," after which you feel refreshed), insomnia (inability to fall and stay asleep), sleep deprivation, and restless legs syndrome impact how long you sleep, how well you sleep, and how much you dream—and they are all far too common. If you faithfully try all the self-help techniques we've provided and you're still not getting 7½ to 9 hours of sound sleep a night on an ongoing basis, it is time to call your doctor.

Your Sleep Trigger

During wakefulness, neurons in the brain stem produce neurotransmitters such as serotonin and norepinephrine that transmit signals to the brain that help it remain in an active awake mode. Other neurons, at the base of the brain, begin signaling when we are ready to fall asleep, and appear to switch off the signals that keep us awake. While we are awake, a chemical called adenosine builds up in our blood, which eventually triggers drowsiness. This chemical then gradually breaks down while we sleep.

Other reasons to call your doctor include:

- You suspect an underlying condition, such as depression or heart failure, is affecting your sleep.
- You snore loudly or make snorting or gasping noises while you sleep.
- You fall asleep doing normal activities, such as talking or driving.
- You don't wake up feeling refreshed and feel fatigued on a regular basis.
- You suspect your medication is causing your sleep problems.

TRAIN YOUR BRAIN TO SLEEP SOUNDLY

The trick to sleeping soundly may be minimizing stress. If you have difficulty sleeping well at night, train your brain to mellow out in the hours leading up to bedtime.

Consider the recent Tel Aviv University study, which found that students who focused on their emotions and anxiety during high-stress periods were more likely to disrupt their sleep than those who tended to ignore their emotions and focus on tasks, effectively turning off their stress and sleeping soundly.

During a routine week of studies, and again during a highly stressful month, researchers documented the sleep patterns of thirty-six students. Sleep quality improved or remained the same for students who directed their focus away from their emotions, while sleep quality diminished for those who fretted and brooded as a way to cope with stress.

If you tend to fret and brood yourself, try to change those habits. Fretting and brooding about anything, especially about things you cannot change, is counterproductive and effectively trains your brain to go down the stress corridor.

Turn That Frown Upside Down

Instead of fretting and brooding, particularly before it's time for your restful sleep, allot yourself fifteen minutes to focus on what's bothering you—and only fifteen minutes. Spend that fifteen minutes working on three lists:

1. List all the terrible things that could go wrong: The Worst-Case Scenario
2. List all the things that might actually happen: The Realistic Scenario
3. List what you can reasonably do to alter the outcome: Your Action Plan

Conclude by spending five minutes breathing and releasing all thoughts, all worries, and all fretting in regards to the matter. Picture a positive outcome and ask your brilliant brain to spend its night connecting all the dots you will need to create a successful outcome. Put a good night's sleep at the top of your action plan, hit the sheets, and make it a habit to use this same tactic for all stress-induced fretting and brooding.

Soon, your brain will begin formulating those lists long before you've reached the fretting and brooding stage, which will help you relinquish the unnecessary fretting and brooding, thereby reducing your stress, improving your sleep, and nourishing your brain.

TO SLEEP, PERCHANCE TO DREAM . . .

Remember, sleep is as good for your emotional health as it is for physical health, because it:

- Is essential to your overall health and well-being.
- Gives your body—and your brain—time to restore, repair, and regenerate.
- Elevates your moods and gives you more energy.

- Makes it easier to handle normal life stressors.
- Helps your brain learn, grow, and master new skills.

Train your brain to get a good night's sleep and you'll be happier. It's that simple. Sweet dreams!

And when you wake up, we'll discuss breakfast and other eating habits that are crucial to your brain's ability to help you get happier!

CHAPTER 9

EAT YOUR WAY TO HAPPINESS

"Life is so brief that we should not glance either too far backwards or forwards . . . therefore study how to fix our happiness in our glass and in our plate."

—Grimod de la Reynière (1758–1838)

A happy brain is a satiated brain . . . and true satiation comes from choosing foods that meet your brain's needs. Consider this: Your brain constitutes about 2 percent of your total body weight, yet it utilizes 20 percent of your body's blood supply. It also utilizes 20 percent of your body's total oxygen supply and 65 percent of its glucose. Those numbers mean your brain requires a host of nutrients in order to remain healthy and function at its peak capacity. Are you feeding your brain what it needs to be happy?

The Happy Eats Quiz

1. You eat according to the food pyramid:
    A. Every meal
    B. Most meals
    C. Only by accident
    D. What pyramid?

2. You eat fast food:
    A. Never
    B. Occasionally
    C. Once or twice a week
    D. Supersize me!

3. **For breakfast, you eat:**
   A. Oatmeal, low-fat milk, and fruit
   B. Bacon and eggs
   C. Coffee and doughnuts
   D. What's breakfast?

4. **When it comes to fats:**
   A. Omega-3 fatty acids are your only source of fats
   B. You limit yourself to "good" fats
   C. Trans fats never pass your lips
   D. What's a trans fat?

5. **Your major sources of protein is/are:**
   A. Low-fat dairy, fish, and legumes
   B. Chicken and fish
   C. Meat
   D. Spam

6. **You drink alcohol:**
   A. Occasionally
   B. A glass of red wine once a day
   C. More than twice a day
   D. Why drink when you can do drugs?

Now tally up your score.

- *If you checked mostly As,* you understand that you have to feed your brain well for it to perform well. But there's always more you can do to keep your brain happy and healthy.
- *If you checked mostly Bs,* you are at least paying attention to what you eat, but there's a lot you can do to feed your little gray cells with better fuel.

- *If you checked mostly Cs,* your lackadaisical attitude toward nutrition is costing you brainpower—power that you need to promote good brain health.
- *If you checked mostly Ds,* you are thwarting your brain health with every bite. You need to adjust your eating and drinking habits if you are to give your brain the nourishment it needs to make you happy.

It doesn't take a neuroscientist to deduce that what you eat plays a vital role in how well your brain functions and how it continues to grow. In fact, the food choices you consume affect virtually every cell, organ, and system in your body. A healthful diet provides your cells with everything they need to function well, reproduce, and repair damage. Unhealthy food choices not only make every cell work harder, they can outright damage your body—and your brain.

Your Brain Comes First

One of the easiest ways to recognize nutrition deficiency is not from a change in body activity but from a change in mental functioning. This is because the frontal lobes, the area of the brain that acts like the CEO of you, are particularly sensitive to falling glucose levels, while brain areas regulating vital functions like breathing, heartbeat, and liver function are more hardy. Researchers at Roehampton University in England noted that, "When your glucose level drops, the symptom is confused thinking, not a change in breathing pattern." Another early sign of a glucose drop is a change in mood, irritability, and overall grumpiness. Keeping your brain well fed keeps it happy!

SIMPLE FOOD CHOICES

The more you know about nutrition, the better, but you don't have to be smarter than a third-grader to understand and incorporate the following extremely basic principle: Some foods are very good for your body (and your brain); other foods, not so much.

Food that improves your health:

- Colorful fruits and vegetables that are rich in antioxidants and fiber
- High-fiber whole-grain foods (brown rice, whole-wheat bread, whole-wheat pasta, and oats)
- Protein (fish, poultry, soy, lean meats, legumes, eggs, low-fat dairy, nuts, and seeds)
- Omega-3 fatty acids found in fish, flaxseed oil, and some nuts
- Nutrient-dense foods (foods in their leanest or lowest-fat forms and without added fats, sugars, starches, or sodium)

Food that has an adverse effect on your health:

- Excess saturated fat (fatty red meat, cheese, ice cream, and fried food)
- Trans fat (margarines, donuts, pies, cakes, chips, and fast food)
- Refined carbohydrates (white rice, white bread, and pasta)
- High-calorie food (containing an excess of solid fats and added sugars, a.k.a. SoFAS*)
- Processed foods (containing an excess of SoFAS)
- Foods with high sodium content
- Beverages with high sugar content (sodas, in particular)

*The United States Department of Agriculture (USDA) reports that Americans typically have 35 percent of their total calories consumed as SoFAS, on average, in contrast to a recommended limit of no more than about 5 to 15 percent of total calories for most individuals.

The U.S. Department of Agriculture's (USDA's) most basic guidelines include (these are pared down for easy digestibility):

- Eat a variety of foods to maximize protein, vitamins, minerals, and fiber.
- Balance the food you eat with physical activity to reduce high blood pressure, heart disease, stroke, certain cancers, and diabetes.
- Choose plenty of whole-grain products, vegetables, and fruits to maximize vitamins, minerals, fiber, and complex carbohydrates.
- Choose a diet low in fat, saturated fat, and cholesterol to reduce risk of heart attack and certain types of cancer, and to maintain a healthy weight.
- Limit sugars because they have little to no nutritive value and can lead to weight gain.
- Limit salt and sodium to reduce your risk of high blood pressure.
- Limit alcohol as it provides no nutritive value and can cause health problems.

Come on, Get Happy!

After assessing data provided by a Gallup World Poll that polled 95 percent of the world's population (more than 150,000 adults in 140 countries), researchers at the University of Kansas established a correlation between happiness and health. Participants reported their emotions, described physical health problems, and answered questions about whether their most basic needs like food, shelter, and personal safety were adequately met. According to the findings, positive emotions were unmistakably linked to better health, and negative emotions were a reliable predator of worse health. Most strikingly, the association between emotional and physical health was more powerful than the connection between health and basic human physical requirements, like adequate nourishment. Even without shelter or food, positive emotions were shown to boost health, even in the poorest countries surveyed.

Eat a Balanced Diet

The USDA consistently researches nutrition and provides a Food Guide Pyramid to help Americans make the healthiest food choices. The pyramid conveys three messages when it comes to choosing food that will meet your nutritional requirements: variety, balance, and moderation. The food groups in the pyramid include the following:

- Whole-grain breads, cereal, rice, and pasta (complex carbohydrates): 6–11 servings
- Fresh vegetables: 3–5 servings
- Fresh fruits: 2–4 servings
- Low-fat or nonfat milk, yogurt, and cheese: 2–3 servings
- Lean meat, poultry, fish, dry beans, eggs, nuts, and meat substitutes: 2–3 servings
- Sweets and fats: use sparingly

Here's the ideal proportion of your food intake: Get 50 percent of your calories from carbohydrates (including fruits and vegetables), 30 percent from protein, and 20 percent from fat.

How Big Is a Serving?

Most people overestimate serving sizes, particularly with the distortions caused by super-sized restaurant meals. Ideally, servings are as follows:

- One serving of whole grains: 1 slice of bread; 1 ounce of ready-to-eat cereal; ½ cup of cooked cereal, rice, or pasta
- One serving of vegetables: 1 cup of raw leafy vegetables; ½ cup of other vegetables, cooked or chopped raw; ¾ cup of vegetable juice
- One serving of fruit: 1 medium apple, banana, or orange; ½ cup of chopped, cooked, or canned fruit; ¾ cup fruit juice
- One serving of dairy: 1 cup of milk or yogurt; 1½ ounces of natural cheese; 2 ounces of processed cheese

- One serving of protein: 3–4 ounces of cooked lean meat, poultry, or fish; ½ cup of cooked dry beans; 2 tablespoons of peanut butter; ⅓ cup of nuts; or 1 egg count as 1 ounce of meat

How Many Calories Should I Eat?

The amount of calories you can eat without adding weight fluctuates depending on your age, gender, and how physically active you are. As you age, your ideal caloric intake declines. To find out your ideal calorie intake, consult with your doctor. In the meantime, consider these as rough guidelines:

- **Adult women** who are sedentary or only mildly active: 1,600 calories per day. Physically active women can add another 600 or so calories. Pregnant women can add even more.
- **Adult men** who are sedentary or only mildly active: 2,200 calories per day. Physically active men can add 600 calories.

How Much Fat Should I Eat?

The USDA recommends that fats should be no more than 30 percent of your total calories. They also recommend consuming no more than 10 percent of that 30 percent from saturated sources of fat, and no more than 7 percent if you have coronary heart disease, diabetes, or high-LDL cholesterol. Using the 30 percent rule, this equates to 53 grams of fat (470 calories) in a 1,600-calorie diet; 73 grams (660 calories) in a 2,200-calorie diet; and 93 grams (830 calories) in a 2,800-calorie diet. Each gram of fat has 9 calories.

THE LOWDOWN ON SUGAR

Sugars are simple carbohydrates that the body uses as a source of energy. During digestion, all carbohydrates break down into sugar, or blood glucose. Some sugars occur naturally, such as in dairy products (as lactose) and fruits (as fructose). Other foods have sugar that is added in processing or preparation. Sugars include white sugar, brown sugar, raw sugar, corn syrup, honey, molasses, maple syrup, and agave. The problem with sugar is that it contains zero nutritive value and way too many calories. If your calorie limit is 1,600 calories per day, you should have no more than 6 teaspoons of sugar; 2,200 calories around 12 teaspoons; and 2,800 calories can go as high as 18 teaspoons. Be very aware that processed foods (soup, boxed rice mixes, sauces, etc.) frequently have "hidden" sugar in that you may not recognize alternative names for sugar, such as crystallized cane juice; evaporated cane juice; maltodextrin (or dextrin); brown rice syrup; and anything ending in "ose," such as fructose, dextrose, lactose, maltose, and so on. All of these indicate added (non-natural) sugar.

Why a Sugar High Leads to a Brain Low

While your brain requires a pretty constant supply of the blood sugar product glucose in order to function properly, constantly eating refined sugars and slurping down sodas does not provide the best route for sugar intake. On the contrary, researchers at the Salk Institute in California found that high glucose levels resulting from quick, easy sugar intake slowly but surely damage cells everywhere in the body, especially those in the brain.

Unfortunately, having too little glucose and having too much glucose are both problematic. When your blood sugar levels drop, your hypothalamus sends out a distress signal that leads to the release of adrenaline to your liver, ordering it to turn excess fat into glucose. When you consume too much sugar, your pancreas secretes insulin to nudge that extra sugar into your cells, and too much insulin can deplete your normal glucose levels, depress your immune system, and lead to kidney disease. Plus, excess insulin also promotes fat storage, which sets up a vicious cycle. Either extreme can leave you feeling woozy, nervous, fatigued, and shaky.

Furthermore, a research group at the University of Wisconsin found that the brain may react to excess refined sugars found in food as if they were a virus or bacteria. The resulting immune response may cause cognitive deficits such as those associated with Alzheimer's disease. Similarly, high blood sugar coupled with performing a mentally challenging task is associated with high levels of cortisol—a stress hormone known to impair memory. In other words, that second (or third) piece of cake at the company birthday party might stress out you, your body, and your brain . . . and affect your afternoon work efficiency!

Those *Were* the Days, My Friend

The average American consumes somewhere between *two to three pounds* of sugar each week. Over the last twenty years, our national sugar consumption exploded from 26 pounds to 135 pounds of sugar—*per person*—annually. Compare that to sugar consumption in the late 1800s, when the average consumption was *five pounds per person—per year*. A time, incidentally, when heart disease and cancer were virtually unknown.

Your Brain on Sugar

It's pretty clear—excessive glucose resulting from too much refined sugar can be very detrimental to your brain, ultimately affecting your attention span, your short-term memory, and your mood stability. Excessive refined sugar can:

- Block membranes and thereby slow down neural communication.
- Increase free radical inflammatory stress on your brain. Free radicals can rupture cells.
- Interfere with synaptic communication.
- Cause neurons to misfire and send erroneous messages that take time and energy to sort out.
- Increase delta, alpha, and theta brain waves, which make it harder to think clearly.
- Can eventually damage your neurons.

Your brain uses 65 percent of your body's glucose, but too much or too little glucose can have a detrimental effect on brain function.

Wondering why soda can cause your brain function to crash and burn? One can of soda contains 10 teaspoons of table sugar, all of which floods into a blood stream that typically contains a total of 4 teaspoons of blood sugar. The rush alerts your pancreas to release a lot of insulin. Some sugar is quickly ushered into the cells, including brain cells, and the rest goes into storage or into fat cells. An hour later, your blood sugar may fall dramatically after the huge insulin rush, creating low blood sugar, and these rapid swings produce symptoms of impaired memory and clouded thinking.

Five Hours of Hell

Those days when you overindulge in sweet confections—be they decadent ice cream, two or three chocolate truffles, a huge slice of blueberry pie, a fistful of peanut butter cookies, or a twelve-ounce soft drink—you potentially trigger a boost in stress hormones that will last the shockingly long time of five hours. Five hours! During this time your body is coping with excess insulin and suffers a depletion of healthy glucose levels. Consider that the next time you feel tempted by sugar-laden confections and maybe settle for a small slice, one teensy scoop, half of a cookie, or just one truffle.

Is There Such a Thing as Healthy Sugars?

Not really . . . a simple sugar is a simple sugar. However, those occurring in real food, such as fructose in fruit and lactose in milk, also provide other nutrients so are slightly more healthy than any other sugar. And even though health food stores love to promote honey, molasses, maple syrup, or agave as natural sweeteners, they are still simple sugars, with the same fattening calories and little nutritive value as refined white sugar. They do, however, tend to be a tad sweeter, so maybe you'll be happier with a smaller amount, but don't kid yourself about them being healthier. Sugar is sugar, and you need to limit how much you consume on a daily basis.

Although honey is a natural sweetener, 96 percent of honey consists of the simple sugars fructose, glucose, and sucrose. Honey also has the highest calorie content of all sugars with 65 calories per tablespoon, compared to the 48 calories per tablespoon found in table sugar. The increased calories are bound to cause increased blood serum fatty acids, as well as weight gain, on top of the risk of more cavities.

WHAT ABOUT SALT?

Although most research has been conducted in adults, the adverse effects of sodium on blood pressure begin early in life. Basically, if you are healthy, you should stay under 1,500 mg. of salt a day (1 teaspoon contains about 2,000 mg.). It's especially important to watch your salt intake if you have high blood pressure, but it's also wise for everyone to limit processed foods, as most are very high in salt content. This includes cured meats, luncheon meats, many cheeses, most canned soups and vegetables, and soy sauce. Always check the sodium content per serving, and if you are eating processed foods, choose those that are lower in salt. After a relatively successful campaign to get consumers to read food labels to spot excessive sugar, food activists are now targeting sodium content, which is massively overboard in many processed foods and in fast food. Read your labels, cook with fresh food, and pare back on salt intake.

If You're Happy, You're Healthy . . . and Vice Versa

Happy people do seem to be healthier, and happiness itself may cause good health. Some studies found that happiness may be as important a factor in overall health as whether or not you smoke. Happiness appears to make people more resistant to serious diseases, like heart disease and strokes, as well as to the common cold. According to a study conducted by Dr. Sheldon Cohen at Carnegie Mellon University, subjects who considered themselves happy were less likely to get sick when exposed to a cold virus—and expressed fewer symptoms even if they did contract the virus.

ALWAYS EAT A HEALTHY BREAKFAST

Your mother was right: Breakfast is one of the most important meals of the day. After a good night's rest, your body—and your brain—needs to replenish its blood sugar stores, which are your body's main source of energy. Your brain in particular needs a fresh supply of glucose each day (because it doesn't store glucose). Tests have shown that breakfast eaters tend to experience better concentration, problem-solving ability, strength, and endurance.

Here are a few healthy suggestions:

- Dry, vitamin-fortified cereal with sliced fruit and skim milk
- Low-fat or nonfat yogurt with fruit or low-fat granola cereal
- Peanut butter on a whole-wheat bagel and orange juice
- A small bran muffin, a banana, and low-fat or skim milk
- Oatmeal with raisins or berries or walnuts (or all three!)
- A breakfast smoothie (blended fruit and skim milk)
- A hard-boiled egg, half a grapefruit, and a slice of whole-grain bread
- Cottage cheese and peaches

Eating a healthy breakfast can help regulate your appetite throughout the day, and even more importantly, research has shown that a high-fiber, low-fat breakfast may play a major contribution in reducing your fat intake for the day. If you have a hard time facing food first thing in the morning, start with a light breakfast, such as a piece of whole-grain toast, a slice of cheese, or fruit. Pack a breakfast or snack to take with you so you can eat once you do get hungry.

FEED IT WELL: FOOD THAT IS GOOD FOR YOUR BRAIN (AND YOUR BODY)

Now that we've discussed basic nutrition, let's discuss food choices that will specifically improve your brain's ability to function, repair, and rejuvenate.

Whole Grains

Whole grains contain various beneficial vitamins, including folate, thiamine, and vitamin B_6, all of which are good for your brain. They also promote healthy blood flow, and more blood flow to your brain gets nutrients there quicker and allows your brain to make the best decisions possible.

Foods made from whole grains should be the base of a nutritious diet. Whole grains can be found in bread, rice, pasta, and oats. Note: Refined grains, such as white breads, white rice, regular pasta, many packaged cereals, and most commercially baked crackers, cookies, bagels, pretzels, and chips, do not contain enough whole-grain fiber to prove beneficial. Whatever nutritious fiber they once had was stripped away during the refinement process. Even if the label claims they are enriched, refined grains are seriously lacking in fiber and nutrition.

Cheerio, Mate!

Cereal grains can be a part of your daily diet as well. They provide much needed fiber, as well as a variety of important vitamins and minerals. Obviously, this refers to low-fat, low-sugar cereals, such as natural granola, oatmeal, bran, bran flakes, and so on. When it comes to your regular fortified cereals, plain Cheerios is among the best options because it offers another source of vitamins and a possibility of slightly lowering your bad cholesterol, without adding too many empty calories.

When buying bread, pasta, rice, crackers, and cereals, always look for the words "whole grain" or "whole wheat" to make sure the product is made from 100 percent whole-wheat flour. To increase your intake of whole-grain foods, look at the ingredient list on the food label and make sure words such as "whole grain," "whole wheat," "rye," "bulgur," "brown rice," "oatmeal," "whole oats," "pearl barley," or "whole-grain corn" appear as one of the first words.

Whole-grain foods supply vitamin E and B vitamins such as folic acid as well as minerals like magnesium, iron, and zinc. Whole grains are also rich in fiber and higher in other important nutrients. In fact, eating plenty of whole-grain breads, bran cereals, and other whole-grain foods can easily provide half of your fiber needs for an entire day.

Tryptophan Is Good for You!

Your body needs the essential amino acid tryptophan to produce serotonin. Luckily, it's found in a wide array of food: turkey, bananas, seeds, tuna, red meat, shellfish, soy, and dairy products. To convert tryptophan to serotonin, combine these foods with those rich in vitamin B_6 and carbohydrates: greens, spinach, turnip, bell peppers, whole grains, beans, and barley. And be sure to choose lean cuts of red meat.

These foods are usually low in fat unless fat is added in processing or preparation, but for maximum benefit, choose grains that are rich in fiber, low in saturated fat, and low in sodium.

Complex Carbohydrates

Carbohydrates are your body's main source of energy, especially for the brain and nervous system. The healthier the carbs you give your body, the better your brain will perform.

Carbohydrates are classified into two different categories: simple carbohydrates (sugars) and complex carbohydrates (starches). Sugars are carbohydrates in their simplest forms (table sugar, honey, jams, candy, syrup, and soft drinks). Some simple sugars, such as naturally occurring sugars, are found in more nutritious foods (fruit and the lactose in dairy products). Complex carbohydrates are basically many simple sugars linked together and can be found in foods such as grains, pasta, rice, vegetables, breads, legumes, nuts, and seeds.

Fiber is also considered a carbohydrate and is important to health. However, fiber is not considered a nutrient because most of it is not digested or absorbed into the body.

Switch Hitters

A new study revealed that switching from white bread, white rice, white noodles, doughnuts, and refined breakfast cereals to oatmeal, brown rice, and 100 percent whole-grain bread and pasta could trim your visceral belly fat by as much as 10 percent. (Visceral fat is the fat that wraps around your other organs and can lead to serious health problems.) That 10 percent could amount to as much as an inch and half off your waist. Not only are the 100 percent whole-grain choices healthier overall, the extra fiber helps your body release a hormone (a glucagon-like peptide 1), that helps you feel more satiated, and increases your sensitivity to insulin, which helps control your blood sugar levels. *Bon appétit!*

Nutrient-Rich Fruits and Vegetables

Leafy green vegetables are brain powerhouses because of all the B vitamins they contain, especially folate. Broccoli, collard greens, Brussels sprouts, kale, and spinach are all superb sources of folate (as are carrots and yams). A study published in the *American Journal of Clinical Nutrition* revealed that eating leafy green vegetables helps keep your brain sharp well into old age.

Fruits and vegetables are also loaded with essential nutrients such as vitamins, minerals, and fiber. Daily requirements for several vitamins—including vitamin C, folic acid, and beta-carotene, the precursor for vitamin A—can be met almost exclusively from fresh vegetables and fruits.

Vegetables

When it comes to vegetables, you can't go wrong with dark green leafy vegetables, such as spinach or broccoli, and dark orange vegetables, such as carrots or yams. Some vegetables also supply sufficient amounts of calcium, iron, and magnesium, and most contain compounds called phytochemicals that may provide additional health benefits.

Color Me Happy!

Scientists at the UCLA Center for Human Nutrition in Los Angeles, California, reported in the November 2001 *Journal of Nutrition* that red and purple foods contain anthocyanins, which are powerful antioxidants. So go crazy for red peppers, eggplant, tomatoes, apples, grapes, blueberries, strawberries, raspberries, and even red wine!

Cruciferous vegetables contain cancer-preventing antioxidant properties (as well as other healthful benefits). The most potent cruciferous vegetables include bok choy (Chinese cabbage), broccoli, Brussels sprouts, cabbage, cauliflower, collard greens, kale, mustard greens, rutabagas, turnips, and watercress. Also high in nutrition are carrots, celery, potatoes, spinach, sweet potatoes, and tomatoes (which contain a cancer-fighting compound known as lycopene).

Combat Free Radicals!

Your brain needs 20–25 percent of your daily intake of oxygen, and while it's percolating throughout the day, firing up brain cells, some oxygen cells go rogue, forming free radicals that can damage your body in a multitude of ways. Since your brain uses the largest part of your body's glucose, free radical oxygen builds up in your brain faster than anywhere else in your body. Having too much of this radical oxygen is particularly damaging to brain cells, creating a sort of biological rust. A lifetime of oxidative insult can lead to diminished brain function. Luckily, phytochemicals and antioxidants stand ready to beat back the radicals—and all you have to do is *eat lots of fruits and vegetables*! Dark green spinach, broccoli rabe, brilliant orange pumpkin, red pomegranates, deep-red raspberries, bright yellow peppers, and other high-intensity, brightly colored fruits and vegetables are packed with highly desirable phytochemicals, while dark-colored fruits and vegetables (dark green, red, and purple foods like spinach, blueberries, eggplants, and purple cabbage) contain antioxidants. Together, these two powerhouse chemicals cut those free radicals off at the pass as well as turn on the genes that boost your body's natural antioxidant system. Go team!

No Longer Svelte

For many years, there was substantial evidence that a traditional Mediterranean diet—one that emphasized breads and other cereal foods made from wheat, vegetables, fruits, nuts, unrefined cereals, olive oil, fish, and wine with meals—was believed slimming because it was lower in saturated fat, meat, and full-fat dairy products. Results from a number of observational studies and clinical trials over a long period of time found that consumption of a traditional Mediterranean diet, defined as one similar to that of a diet people living in Crete in the 1960s would have eaten, was associated with one of the lowest risks of coronary heart disease in the world. Sadly, modern times have come to Crete, and the infamous Mediterranean diet now includes increased saturated fat and cholesterol, and reduced intake of the somewhat healthier monounsaturated fats. These trends have been accompanied by a steady rise in weight and heart disease risk.

Fruits

When it comes to fruit, eating a variety ensures a greater intake of these essential nutrients, and choosing different types and colors is a good way to go. Fruit is full of healthy substances such as vitamin C, vitamin A, potassium, folic acid, antioxidants, phytochemicals, and fiber, just to name a few. Citrus fruits, berries, and melons are excellent sources of vitamin C. Dried fruits are available all year long and are an excellent source of many nutrients and fiber. Apples, bananas, berries, citrus fruit, and melons are also nutrient- and fiber-rich.

Lean Protein

Protein is also vitally important because your body requires it to build and repair bone, muscles, connective tissue, skin, internal organs, and blood. Hormones, antibodies, and enzymes, which regulate your body's chemical reactions, are all composed of protein. As far as benefiting your brain, dopamine and norepinephrine require tyrosine to be made (much like serotonin requires tryptophan), which comes almost exclusively from proteins. Also, tryptophan is almost exclusively found in meat, eggs, and dairy.

Protein can also be used as an energy source, if your carbohydrates fall short. However, this is not an ideal choice for the brain, as it will burn energy more quickly and steal resources usually reserved for cellular metabolism.

It's found in meat, poultry, fish, eggs, milk, cheese, yogurt, and soy products. Legumes, seeds, and nuts also supply some protein. Since animal products provide the majority of protein, choose lower-fat dairy products and lean cuts of meat.

Do You Know How Much Protein Is Enough?

It's probably a lot less than you imagine. According to the USDA, males aged nineteen to twenty-four require 58 grams, while those over twenty-five require 63 grams. Females aged nineteen to twenty-four require 46 grams, while those over twenty-four require 50 grams. Pregnant women require 60 grams; breast-feeding women require 65 grams in the first six months and 62 grams in the following months, until they cease breast-feeding. All those numbers mean that it's easy to meet your protein needs. Here's a list that will give you an idea of protein grams and serving sizes:

- 1 3- to 4-ounce serving of lean meat, poultry, or fish contains about 25–35 grams of protein per day. That serving is approximately the size of a deck of cards.
- 1 cup of cooked beans or lentils contains about 18 grams of protein.

- 1 cup of low-fat or fat-free milk contains 8 grams of protein.
- 1 cup of low-fat yogurt contains about 10 grams of protein.
- 1 cup of low-fat cottage cheese contains about 28 grams of protein.
- 2 tablespoons of peanut butter contains about 7 grams of protein.
- 2 ounces of low-fat cheese contains about 14–16 grams of protein.
- 1 medium egg contains about 7 grams of protein.
- 1 serving of vegetables contains around 1–3 grams of protein.
- 1 serving of grain foods generally contains 3–6 grams of protein.

Dairy: Milk, Yogurt, and Cheese

Yes, you still need milk—or at least milk products—even after you grow as tall or taller than your parents. Milk, yogurt, and cheese, in particular, provide protein and many essential vitamins and minerals, such as calcium, riboflavin, phosphorus, potassium, vitamin A, and most especially vitamin D.

Depression and Diabetes

Studies have shown that depressed adults are 60 percent more likely to have type 2 diabetes. Researchers theorize that the stress hormone cortisol, which can be associated with depression, raises blood sugar levels. See your doctor if you suspect this is happening to you.

Vitamin D receptors are found throughout the brain and especially in the hippocampus, and low vitamin D levels have been linked to poor memory and cognitive function. Vitamin D also aids in the growth of new neurons and neurotransmitter synthesis.

Unfortunately, dairy products also contain saturated fat and cholesterol, so choose the lowest fat you can bear and keep portions small.

The USDA Food Pyramid suggests consuming two to three servings from the milk group each day. Keep in mind that one serving is likely much smaller than you imagine. They equate one serving to:

- 1 cup low-fat or fat-free milk
- ⅓ cup dry milk
- 1½ ounces natural cheese
- 2 ounces processed cheese
- 1 cup low-fat yogurt
- ¾ cup low-fat cottage cheese

The Skinny on Fats

Fats are also vital to a healthy diet. Fats help carry, absorb, and store the fat-soluble vitamins (A, D, E, and K) in your bloodstream. Fats also help regulate your body temperate. Having some body fat cushions your organs and protects them from injury. However, as you probably already know, there are good fats and bad fats for both your body and your brain.

Not Just Popeye's Girlfriend

If you grew up watching Popeye fight battles to protect his beloved Olive Oyl, you'll enjoy the fact that olive oil is widely accepted as one of the good fats. It's high in monounsaturated fats, which helps reduce LDL (the "bad" cholesterol), and studies have shown that people who consume olive oil, in preference to other fats, have a lower incidence of heart disease.

The good fats, or lipids, that work so beautifully in your body—and your brain—are called fatty acids. Essential fatty acids cannot be manufactured in your body so must come from the foods you eat (or supplements you take, although food sourcing is highly preferable). As far as your body, fatty acids are primarily used to produce hormone-like substances that regulate a wide range of functions, including blood pressure, blood clotting, blood lipid levels, the immune response, and the inflammation response to injury or infection.

Approximately 60 percent of your brain matter consists of fats that create all the cell membranes in the body. Let's review: The good fat in your brain matter creates all the cell membranes in your body! If your diet is loaded with bad fats, your brain can only make low-quality nerve cell membranes that don't function well; if your diet provides the essential, good fats, your brain cells can manufacture higher-quality nerve cell membranes and influence positively your nerve cells' ability to function at their peak capacity. (Magnesium also plays a critical role in nerve cell development and optimal functioning.)

Thus, it's important to choose foods that offer the essential fatty acids your body and brain need. Unfortunately, even good fats are a very concentrated source of energy, providing more than double the amount of calories in one gram of carbohydrate or protein, which is why it's important to choose the healthy fats and to eat them in moderation.

Omega-3 Fatty Acids

Omega-3 fatty acids are great for mental clarity, concentration, and focus. In fact, omega-3 fatty acids seem to be particularly important for brain health in children and adolescents. In 2010, a multinational research group found that omega-3 fatty acids may help to prevent psychiatric disorders in children. Somewhat alarmingly, the typical American child has a diet bereft of omega-3 fatty acids. Purdue researchers have linked this deficit to a higher risk of attention deficit disorder and other learning disabilities.

Omega-3 fatty acids play an essential role throughout your life and should be at the top of your shopping list in terms of positive value for your brain. However, they are fattening so maximizing the sources in terms of benefits as opposed to caloric content is a wise move. Certain foods containing omega-3 fatty acids are especially good for your brain. These include:

- Certain cold-water fish (bluefish, herring, mackerel, rainbow trout, salmon, sardines, tuna, and whitefish)
- Olive oil
- Flaxseed oil
- Peanut oil
- Canola oil

Researchers at Harvard University suggest that omega-3 fats (which are also available in supplements, though food sources are preferred) may disrupt the brain signals that trigger the characteristic mood swings seen with bipolar disorder. If these findings hold true in future studies, omega-3 fatty acids may have implications for successfully treating other psychiatric disorders such as depression and schizophrenia. Caution: No one with these disorders should attempt to self-medicate. Always consult with your doctors before adding supplements.

Why Your Heart Loves Omega-3s

Omega-3 fatty acids may decrease the risk of stroke and heart attack, as well as protect against abnormal heart rhythms, the leading cause of death after heart attacks. Omega-3 fatty acids may provide protection by enhancing the stability of the heart cells and increasing their resistance to becoming overexcited. Eating fish just one to two times per week has shown a 40 percent reduction in sudden deaths from cardiac arrhythmias.

LIMIT SATURATED AND HYDROGENATED FATS

Essential fatty acids are the most important nutrients for your brain, but most American diets are sadly lacking in these "good" essential fats (found in flaxseed oil, olive oil, and fish oil) and way over the top when it comes to saturated, hydrogenated, and partially hydrogenated trans fats. You can easily recognize the "bad" fats (saturated and processed fats), as they're the ones that have been processed or hydrogenated and remain solid when refrigerated. They are typically found in:

- Commercial baked goods: pies, cakes, doughnuts, cookies, etc.
- Processed foods and fast foods
- Fatty cuts of beef, pork, and lamb
- Butter, margarines
- Whole milk, ice cream
- Cheese
- Crackers, potato chips, corn chips, cheese puffs, pretzels, etc.
- Candy
- Mayonnaise and some salad dressings
- Palm, palm kernel, and coconut oils

When unsaturated fats are heated for a long time, in metal pots and pans, they form altered or trans fatty acids. In contrast to healthy fatty acids (whose soft pliability helps nerve cell membranes function smoothly), these trans fatty acids become double-bonded, rigid, and thus tend to gum up synaptic or electrical nerve cell communication. Besides greatly increasing your chance of gaining too much weight on foods that contain little to zero nutritional value, here's a short list of the damage trans fats can do to your body and brain:

- Alter the synthesis of neurotransmitters, such as dopamine.
- Increase LDL (bad) cholesterol and decrease HDL (good) cholesterol.
- Increase the amount of plaque in blood vessels and increase the possibility of blood clots forming, both of which puts your heart—and your brain—at risk.
- Increase the amount of triglycerides in your system, which slows down the amount of oxygen going to your brain, and the excess of which has been linked to depression.

One reason America has become a nation of overweight people is that our consumption of essential fatty acids has declined by more than 80 percent while our consumption of trans fats has skyrocketed more than 2,500 percent! If you want your brain to be healthy and happy, severely limit saturated and hydrogenated fats.

Two More, Huge Reasons to Ban Trans Fats

Trans fats may be even more harmful than saturated and hydrogenated fats. Saturated fats tend to raise cholesterol levels and thus endanger your heart and your brain, but trans fats can be far worse. Here are two reasons you may want to ban trans fats from your diet:

1. Trans fat works against your brain by disrupting the production of energy in the mitochondria (the energy factories) of brain cells.
2. When your diet is high in trans fatty acids and low in omega-3 fatty acids, your brain absorbs twice as many trans fatty acids.

When it comes to trans fats, just say no!

CAFFEINE

No, caffeine isn't its own food group, despite what some exhausted people might say. Coffee may be the most popular drug in America; some 85 percent of Americans confess to drinking coffee daily. We love our coffee because its high caffeine content serves as a relatively fast-acting stimulant. So what if it temporarily increases your heart rate and blood pressure? It wakes us up, wakes our brains up, helps us focus, and boosts the production of serotonin in our brains. Sure, too much can leave you jittery and nervous, and too much can prematurely age your brain because it dehydrates and reduces blood flow, but it tastes so good.

It's also true that consuming too much caffeine can irritate your stomach, cause headaches, create anxiety, serve as a diuretic, and disturb your sleep. And it's important to note that caffeine is not only found in coffee beans but also in tea leaves, cocoa beans, and products derived from these sources. You may not be aware that caffeine is also found in more than a thousand different over-the-counter and prescription drugs and that there is a very small amount of caffeine in decaffeinated coffee.

So How Much Is Too Much?

Unless you're a massive coffee drinker (or consuming caffeine from a multitude of known and hidden sources), as long as you still drink plenty of healthy beverages, such as water, fruit juice, milk, or green tea, you can have a few cups of coffee and feel perfectly good about it. However, the caffeine you find in coffee (and in chocolate, some soft drinks, some medications, and black tea) is a psychoactive drug, that is, it alters your mood, and consuming too much can become a problem and cause withdrawal problems if you abruptly stop.

Save the Philosophizing for Later

Downing those cups of coffee in the morning may fire up your neurons, but the general consensus derived from caffeine studies shows that it can increase the output and quality of your work, but only if the work you're doing doesn't require nuance or abstract thinking. Caffeine seems to speed your thinking processes up a bit, and improve memory creation and retention when it comes to declarative memory, the kind you use when memorizing lists. But thanks to the increasing tolerance that comes with regular consumption, it eventually takes more and more caffeine to get the same effect.

Like every other food or drink, the portion sizes of coffee can be misleading. Most coffee mugs, for example, actually contain two to two and half cups, and the fancy sizes at your favorite coffee places can hold a lot more coffee than you think. The pharmacological active dose of caffeine is defined as 200 milligrams, and the daily recommended not-to-exceed intake level is the equivalent of one to three cups of coffee per day (139 to 417 milligrams). Below is a guideline for approximate amounts of caffeine in commonly used foods and beverages:

- Coffee, brewed from ground beans—6 oz. = 100 mg.
- Tea, brewed from whole leaves—6 oz. = 10–50 mg.
- Cola, can or bottle—12 oz. = 50 mg.
- Cocoa, as milk chocolate bar—1 oz. = 6 mg.
- One cup of semisweet chocolate chips = 92 mg.

ALCOHOL

Sitting back and relaxing with friends while enjoying a beer or a glass of wine are socializing events many people enjoy. Studies have even extolled *some* of the virtues of alcohol, especially red wine, which has been shown to have antioxidant properties. (Some studies show that a single glass with dinner can actually boost your brainpower!)

Beware of Mixing Alcohol and Caffeine

In November 2010, the Federal Trade Commission (FTC) issued a strong warning that caffeinated alcoholic beverages posed a "significant risk" to consumer health. The statement noted that inexperienced drinkers "may not realize how much alcohol they have consumed because caffeine can mask the sense of intoxication." It's wise to read labels carefully and steer clear of alcoholic beverages that include caffeine.

However, when one glass of wine becomes three or four, or one beer becomes a six-pack, these possible good benefits disappear entirely, to be replaced with negative consequences for your brain and its ability to do its job. It doesn't take a huge amount of alcohol before you'll have difficulty walking, talking, or responding. Blurred vision, slurred speech, slowed reaction times, and impaired memory are among the many immediate consequences of excessive consumption.

Your Brain on Alcohol

Clearly, alcohol affects your brain, even in the short term. The long-term effects on the brain of too much alcohol consumption are much worse and include:

- Blackouts
- Permanent memory lapses
- Nerve damage
- Brain shrinkage
- Vitamin B$_1$ (thiamine) deficiency
- Alternations in the balance of neurotransmitters such as GABA
- Serious alcohol consumption on a regular basis can also lead to several debilitating brain disorders

YOUR BRAIN ON DRUGS

Yes, we're using the now trite line from a series of famous commercials in which an actor dropped eggs into a frying pan to warn about drugs' adverse effects on your brain. Those ads, along with Nancy Reagan's slogan to Just Say No, were designed to turn people off to drugs. Did they work? Not if you count the millions of people all over the world who are currently affected by addiction to drugs: from something as simple as lighting up a cigarette to something as iconically dangerous as inserting a needle into your arm to administer heroin.

Different types of drugs affect your brain in different ways. Some, like cocaine and amphetamines, directly bind to different kinds of dopamine receptors, creating a burst of pleasure and creating a frantic, awake, energetic feeling. Others, like heroin and many addictive painkillers, such as morphine, are opiates that take over your internal opioid system, yielding a feeling of relaxed euphoria. Nicotine binds to your acetylcholine receptors and is often thought to increase feelings of alertness and calm.

Many other types of drugs trick your brain into altering its neurochemistry, and these changes can be debilitating and permanent, resulting in habituation, tolerance, and addiction. The feelings of momentary happiness, when pursued on a regular basis, are followed by painful withdrawal symptoms, including anxiety and often physical pain, when the drug is no longer in the system and the brain scrambles to compensate.

Drugs, such as cocaine, boost dopamine release, but continued use ends up depleting the brain's natural supply of dopamine. This means that, eventually, the person taking cocaine on a regular basis doesn't have enough dopamine without cocaine, which leads to a constant desire for cocaine.

THE BAD NEWS ABOUT FOOD CRAVINGS: IT *IS* ALL IN YOUR HEAD

You've probably experienced something similar to the following scenario:

You're sitting at your desk at work, mind only partially absorbed by a tedious project. Then, out of nowhere, a thought strikes your brain like a Mack truck: pizza! Even if you normally limit pizza to those occasions when you're with your family or friends, once or twice a month at most, you are suddenly feeling an insane urge for pizza. You can smell the melting cheese and taste the scrumptious sausage and spicy pepperoni so vividly your tongue tingles at the thought of a greasy pizza from your favorite corner dive. Although you were planning a dinner of grilled chicken and veggies, your plans have changed. You *must* have pizza. Now!

Sound familiar? Moments of cravings can strike out of the blue and linger for hours. You may not even be particularly *hungry* when the craving strikes, and do you know why? It's because the signal for the particular food craving is usually not coming from your stomach. It's being faxed straight down from your brain, overriding your stomach's hunger signals and holding you captive to the thought of that corner dive's greasy pizza.

Give Me Chocolate . . . Now!
Just about everyone gets food cravings, but women seem to have it worse. Surveys conducted at the Monell Chemical Senses Center found that nearly 100 percent of females and 70 percent of males in their study had experienced at least one strong food craving in 2009. Women tended to crave sweeter foods—anything chocolate being number one for most—while men tended towards the savory, like barbecue ribs and French fries. For both sexes, the usual foods that lure us in are those rich in fat or calories.

So What's the Deal with Cravings?

Unfortunately, when it comes to crazy cravings, your stomach is blameless. Most of your gut peptides and chemicals are only concerned with whether or not they are full. Your stomach is responsible for hunger; your brain is responsible for food cravings. And sadly, a "mind hunger" for fat and high-calorie treats isn't entirely necessary for survival.

In fact, scientists have largely debunked the theory that food cravings are our bodies' ways of nagging us to eat a specific type of nutrient. The fact is high-calorie and high-fat foods tend to trigger the release of chemicals called opioids, which can give a sense of euphoria—and who doesn't crave a little euphoria?

Your Brain on a Food Craving

When study participants at the University of Pennsylvania were asked to think about a favorite food, brain areas such as the caudate (which provides a rich source of brain dopamine) and the hippocampus (triggering memory) would light up. The type of dopamine stimulation and chemical reward that we obtain from fulfilling food cravings has been compared to drug addiction because both behaviors follow similar neural pathways. Fulfilling food cravings is very similar to what drug addicts experience when they get high, except it's a milder form of chemical stimulation.

Neurologically speaking, those greasy, fat-pushing, fast-food joints aren't much different from your neighborhood drug pusher. Furthermore, just like drug addicts, someone who continually eats chocolate (as an example) raises their chocolate threshold, which means that they gradually need to eat more and more brownies to regain the level of their initial pleasure.

But Don't We Need Certain Foods?

Some food psychologists believe that our innate food cravings evolved as a way to ensure that our bodies got enough energy. Granted, much of what we desire is fattening or high in calories, which often translates to obesity today. But back in the time of hunters and gatherers, such energy-dense food was necessary to provide enough energy for the men and women doing hard labor to survive until his or her next meal. Furthermore, most of our modern food cravings are likely associated with feelings of good times, times spent sharing meals with friends or families. Your unrepentant craving for chocolate chip cookies likely stems from those deliciously sweet, lazy afternoons spent making them with your mom.

When it comes to food cravings, some nutritionists still recommend substitution: When you crave a brownie, eat a nice, crispy healthy apple instead! But sometimes, resisting the urge just doesn't work. In fact, resisting the urge may lead to overeating when you do succumb. That's why most psychologists and nutritionists now advise giving in to cravings on occasion. The key is limiting the frequency and the amount. If you're craving chocolate, go ahead and have a piece . . . or two small pieces at most. If you want a cheeseburger, split it with a friend.

And, most importantly, make new, positive memories of eating healthfully with friends and family. Sharing good times over nutritious food will associate those new, happy memories with the food on the table, and it may be that, not too long in the future, you'll be struck with a sudden, overwhelming urge for some nice yogurt with blueberry topping. Now that's training your brain to be happy!

EAT YOUR WAY TO A HEALTHY BODY AND BRAIN

What you eat has everything to do with how your body functions and its ability to repair and generate new cells. If you want to maintain your health, it's important to follow the nutritional guidelines provided in this chapter (or provided by your physician), making sure your body receives the nutrients it needs. If you want to give your brain a power boost, it certainly makes sense to choose foods that have been proven to benefit the brain.

All the recommended foods in this chapter are easily available, and most are affordable. We'll touch on superfoods and supplements in the next chapter, but always remember that it's always better to get your nutrients right from their natural sources, to rely on whole grains, lean protein, fresh fruits and vegetables, and healthy fats . . . and to prepare your foods at home rather than eating processed foods.

Eat lots of whole grains, lots of fruits and vegetables, a limited amount of lean protein, a limited amount of dairy, and a severely limited amount of good fats. Choose those that will provide the most nutrients for the least calories, and you'll be svelte, healthy, and happy!

Now we'll move on to discussing the superfoods you can add to your diet to make your brain even happier.

CHAPTER 10

BOOST YOUR WAY TO HAPPINESS:
Brain Superfoods

"Of course, there are more than just 10 'superfoods.' In fact, just about every brightly colored fruit and vegetable fits the category of a superfood, as do nuts, beans, seeds and aromatic and brightly colored herbs and spices. The beneficial properties of each one of these superfoods could fill an entire book."

—Dr. Nicholas Perricone

SUPERFOODS FOR SUPER BRAIN PERFORMANCE

Now that we've covered basic nutrition and offered suggestions for you to vastly improve your eating habits to more fully nurture your body and your brain, it's time to cover the superfoods that can give your brain that extra boost.

In nutritional circles, miracle foods that offer extraordinary improvements for your body are called *superfoods* because they provide essential nutrients. A healthy diet containing a variety of superfoods helps you maintain your weight, fight disease, live longer, and function at your peak capacity. And when your brain is functioning at its peak capacity, it'll be easier for you to train it to be happy!

Note: All the following superfoods are "real" foods, as opposed to processed foods, and all are readily available at your local supermarket.

FISH

Fish is loaded with omega-3 fatty acids, as well as protein, vitamins, and minerals. Hundreds of studies have shown that these omega-3s may provide benefits that include battling cancer, asthma, depression, cardiovascular disease, ADHD, and autoimmune disease. The omega-3 fatty acids found in fish have also been shown to be particularly good for your brain. A study of 2,000 Norwegians, aged seventy to seventy-four, found that those who ate fish of any kind were two to three times less likely to perform poorly on cognitive tests.

Salmon Gone Wild

Salmon has its own perch (pun intended) when it comes to being a brain superfood, but it's important that you choose wild salmon rather than farm-raised salmon. Farm-raised salmon is often injected with antibiotics and often contains 70 percent more fat than wild salmon, and 200 percent more fat than wild Pacific pink salmon and chum salmon. Wild salmon is drug-free and also has higher levels of the beneficial omega-3 fatty acids. So go wild when it comes to salmon, and your brain will love you for it!

The USDA and the American Heart Association recommend eating two eight-ounce servings of fish per week. Yet they also caution against eating too much seafood, particularly if it has a higher level of mercury content. For seafood that is higher in mercury content—shark, swordfish, king mackerel, tilefish, canned albacore (white) tuna, tuna steaks, lobster, halibut, and orange roughy—they caution against eating more than one six-ounce serving, which is about the size of two decks of cards for thicker cuts or two checkbooks for thinner cuts.

Seafood lower in mercury include shrimp, canned light tuna (not albacore tuna), salmon, pollock, catfish, cod, crab, flounder/sole, grouper, haddock, herring, mahi-mahi, ocean perch, oysters, rainbow trout, sardines, scallops, shrimp, spiny lobster, tilapia, and trout.

In the last century, Americans drastically reduced their intake of essential fish oils, and the deficit that results from eating way too many processed foods and less fish, scientists agree, has contributed to an epidemic of heart disease. A spate of studies has also linked low fish consumption to high rates of major depression, bipolar disorder, postpartum depression, and suicidal tendencies.

How Omega-3s Can Help Depression

In regards to major depression, omega-3s appear to help in part by making it easier for the receptors on brain cells to process mood-related signals from neighboring neurons. In regards to bipolar disorder, omega-3s seem to inhibit, or calm, a process called signal transduction, which tends to misfire and send confusing signals in bipolar brains. When psychiatrist Andrew Stoll supplemented the medications of thirty bipolar patients with either 10 grams of omega-3s or a placebo, those receiving the fish oil did so much better he switched the controls over to fish oil after four months into a nine-month trial. Even though nutritionists and scientists agree that further studies are needed, it's important to note that studies have not found any adverse side effects to omega-3s. "Omega-3s just give back to the body what it requires for proper functioning," reported Stoll.

Why Pregnant and New Mothers Need Omega-3s

While omega-3s are important for everyone, an adequate supply is especially critical for infants and mothers. Gestating and newborn (breast-fed) babies often deplete their mothers of these fats, which could set the stage for postpartum depression. A gestating baby consumes large amounts of these fats during the third trimester of gestation and acquires a steady supply through breast milk following birth. Infant formulas, by contrast, deliver very little omega-3s. (The World Health Organization recommends supplementing formulas with omega-3s, and the U.S. FDA approved these formulas in 2006, with the caveat that the FDA expects infant formula manufacturers to pursue rigorous postmarketing surveillance and monitoring of formulas containing omega-3s.)

BLUEBERRIES

When it comes to brain protection, there's nothing quite like blueberries. Among its treasures are antioxidant and anti-inflammatory compounds, which some studies indicate may offer potential for reversing short-term memory loss and forestalling many other effects of aging. In a study on reversing memory loss reported in the *Wall Street Journal*, blueberries had the strongest impact on the mental function of aging rodents than any of the other fruits tested.

Miracle Berries
The reason berries are so nutritious and good for the brain is because their colorful skins contain flavonoids, which have been shown to have antioxidant abilities. Flavonoids are also found in green tea, soy, apples, and cherries, but they are most potent in red and purple fruits. Other berries that are potent antioxidants for your brain are acai berries, goji berries, mulberries, boysenberries, and cranberries. The fruits with the highest capacity to absorb free radicals are (in order of potency): blueberries, blackberries, strawberries, raspberries, and plums.

Plus, blueberries have 38 percent more antioxidants than red wine. One cup of blueberries reportedly provides three to five times the antioxidants as five servings of carrots, broccoli, squash, and apples. What this means for your health is a lower risk of heart disease; vibrant, firm skin; and a boost in brain power. Eat them spring, summer, winter, and fall. Eat them frozen in smoothies or mixed with yogurt and walnuts as a real brain pleaser.

APPLES

The active ingredient in apple pulp is pectin, a soluble form of fiber that may be effective against heart disease and stroke because it helps reduce "bad" cholesterol by keeping it in the intestinal tract until it is eliminated. A study published in the *Journal of the National Cancer Institute* shows that pectin binds certain cancer-causing compounds in the colon, accelerating their removal from the body. European studies indicate that apple pectin can help to eliminate lead, mercury, and other toxic heavy metals from the human body—so "an apple a day" is especially good advice for those living in polluted areas.

Why Your Skin Loves Apples

Apples are not only good for your brain; they can also have a significant effect on how well your skin ages. Australian researchers discovered that skin wrinkling in older people (due to overexposure to the sun) may be positively influenced by a diet high in vegetables, legumes, olive oil, fruits (particularly apples), and tea.

NUTS

Nuts are high in fat but also supply the good fats, as well as minerals, fiber, and protein. Walnuts, almonds, hazelnuts, and pecans all pack healthy mono- and polyunsaturated fats that help keep your arteries clear, which helps blood and oxygen flow freely to your brain. Major bonus: Nuts also provide the raw materials your body uses to produce mood-boosting serotonin in your brain, and they also contain magnesium, which helps to insulate your nerve fibers to help them fire faster and with more efficiency. Thus, you will get better-working, happier neurons!

Yes, nuts are high in calories from fat, so you can't gobble them down by the handful. Try a tablespoon or two sprinkled on foods high in vitamin C, such as fruit and vegetables (because the vitamin C increases the body's absorption of the iron in nuts), or on your cooked oatmeal.

Excess salt can also be a problem when consuming nuts, so look for nuts that are unsalted. It's not important whether they are roasted or unroasted, but candy-coated is never a good idea.

Because they contain high-caloric fat, it's important to eat nuts in moderation—one ounce or about twelve walnut halves or twenty-four almonds. Spread them throughout the day for little protein and fat pick-me-ups. Eating more is fine, as long as you pare down fat calories elsewhere in your diet. Another good idea: For a light snack, try mixing chopped walnuts and almonds with dried fruit, figs, or raisins, which are rich in potassium.

QUINOA

Once known as "the gold of the Incas," this hearty little grainlike crop has more protein, iron, and unsaturated fats and fewer carbohydrates than any real grain on the market. (Quinoa isn't a grain because it's not a member of the grass family.) A complete protein, quinoa provides ten essential amino acids and is packed with minerals, B vitamins, and fiber. It's considered a superfood because it contains high amounts of the amino acid lysine, which is essential for tissue growth and repair. It's a great source of manganese as well as magnesium, iron, copper, phosphorous, and the B vitamins, especially folate, another essential nutrient needed for the formation and development of new and normal body tissue. (Your body cannot make folate, so it must be obtained from foods and supplements.)

Eggs ... actly

First eggs were good, and then they were bad . . . and now they're good again, sort of. Basically, an egg has protein (in the white part), fat (in the yellow part), but no carbohydrates. The white has a few other nutrients, while the yellow has a high amount of vitamin B_{12}

and folate. For a while we were told to avoid the yolk because it held the fat that created cholesterol, but now nutritionists say the fat in an egg is good for the brain and doesn't contribute to higher levels of cholesterol in the blood. Still, the FDA's latest guidelines caution against eating more than seven eggs a week. That means one a day can't be bad!

The other B vitamin quinoa provides is riboflavin, or B_2, which is necessary for the proper production of cellular energy in your body. By improving the energy metabolism within the brain and muscle cells, B_2 may help reduce the frequency of migraine attacks. It also has high amounts of potassium and magnesium that help lower your blood pressure and strengthen your heart.

It's Alive!

That bulge around your middle, a.k.a. the dreaded belly fat, is far more than simply unattractive. In addition to the bulge, it also lodges unseen visceral fat around your heart and other vital organs, and it eventually takes on a life of its own. That's right: belly fat cells are capable of producing their own hormones, and they release cytokines, the same inflammatory chemicals that your body releases when it needs to ward off an infection or heal from an injury. These cytokines have been linked to depression, decreased ability for long-term memory, and may lower your brain-derived neurotrophic factor (BDNF), a protein that helps support existing neurons and encourages the growth and differentiation of new neurons and synapses, also known as the highly desired plasticity.

OATS

Oats are a marvelous source of energy, and oat bran is an excellent fiber that can reduce serum cholesterol. Whether you choose steel-cut oats (the most roughly cut and least processed), rolled or "old-fashioned" oats, quick oats, or instant, all types of oats are effective at reducing cholesterol. To get the daily 3 grams of soluble fiber recommended for cholesterol lowering, you'll need to eat 2 ounces of oat bran (⅔ cup dry or about 1½ cups cooked) or 3 ounces of oatmeal (1 cup dry or 2 cups cooked). As an alternative, sprinkle oat bran on cereal and yogurt, or add it to toppings for fruit crisps and casseroles. You can also use oat bran to coat chicken, lean meats, or fish before baking, or add it to meat loaf or meatballs in place of some of the breadcrumbs.

SOY

According to nutritional experts, soy protein appears to lower blood cholesterol levels, decreasing blood clots and platelet clumping, both of which can increase the risk for a heart attack or stroke. Soy also improves the elasticity of arteries, which makes blood flow better, and reduces oxidation of low-density lipoprotein (LDL or "bad" cholesterol), which can lower the risk of plaque formation. Soy can be found in edamame (green soy beans), mature soy beans, soy nuts, soy milk, tofu (coagulated soy), tempeh (fermented soybean cake), soy sauce, and miso (fermented soy). There are also soy-based cheeses and dairy products, as well as soy bean oil.

Adding just one serving a day of soy can make a difference. Note: If you have a family member who has had breast cancer, check with your doctor before adding a lot of soy to your diet.

CHOCOLATE

In a study done by Salk Institute researcher Henriette van Praag and colleagues, a compound found in cocoa, epicatechin, combined with exercise, was found to promote functional changes in a part of the brain involved in the formation of learning and memory. Epicatechin is one of a group of chemicals called flavonols, which have previously been shown to improve cardiovascular function and increase blood flow to the brain.

Plug Up the Brain Drains

Some foods are known to interfere with healthy brain functioning. Specifically, it's always wise to limit alcohol, sugar, aspartame sweetener, and MSG. Alcohol makes you dull; sugar makes you foggy; aspartame and MSG are brain excitotoxins and can lead to brain cell death. Also avoid processed foods that are loaded with sugar, additives, or stimulants, as they tend to worsen depression symptoms. Instead, stick to foods that are good for your brain and make you happy as a bonus.

Why Chocolate Helps Make Your Brain Happy

- It contains serotonin, which can elevate your mood.
- It contains phenethylamine (PEA), a neurotransmitter your neurons release when you feel euphoric. PEA stimulates anandamide, a neurotransmitter that both provides a natural high and calms your neurological system, reducing anxiety.
- It contains flavonoids (plant pigments) that are responsible for antioxidant activity and help protect your good cholesterol and arterial linings. Flavonoids also prevent blood platelets from aggregating, similar to the effect aspirin has on your body. There have also been studies indicating that the flavonoids in cocoa inhibit an enzyme that causes inflammation.
- It contains arginine, an amino acid that stimulates nitric acid, which helps your blood vessels dilate, serving as a natural anti-inflammatory, regulating blood pressure and blood flow.

- It contains theobromine, caffeine, and other substances that can improve concentration and focus.
- It contains phytochemicals, which increase your body's ability to block arterial damage caused by free radicals and inhibit platelet aggregation, which could cause a heart attack or stroke.

So Go Ahead, Indulge in Chocolate . . . Occasionally

Dark, semisweet chocolate is the best chocolate in terms of nutritive value. Milk chocolate typically has modified milk ingredients and way too much saturated fat and sugar. Instead, look for organic or fair-trade dark chocolate (cacao beans should be listed as an ingredient) with 70 percent, or more, cocoa. If the chocolate has been sweetened with raw organic sugar cane or honey, that's a plus. You can eat two or three small squares and feel confident you're doing something good for your body and brain, but it's wise to limit your indulgence to no more than three times a week.

As If You Need Another Reason to Eat Chocolate

According to study results published in the American Chemical Society's *Journal of Agriculture and Food Chemistry*, cocoa powder has nearly twice the antioxidants of red wine and up to three times that found in green tea. In fact, dark chocolate tested higher for antioxidants than fruits and vegetables. Its closest competitor, milk chocolate, came in second, and prunes came in third.

FINE-TUNING NUTRITION

Now that we've gone from general nutrition to brain superfoods, it's time to get down to the real nitty-gritty and discuss vitamins and supplements that can improve your brain health and thus lead to greater happiness.

CHAPTER 11

SUPPLEMENT YOUR WAY TO HAPPINESS: Vitamins and Minerals That Boost Brainpower

"All those vitamins aren't to keep death at bay, they're to keep deterioration at bay."

—Jeanne Moreau

"Vitamins, minerals and other supplements won't compensate for a poor diet, but they can help fill nutritional gaps in a good one."

—Dr. Andrew Weil

THE ROLE VITAMINS PLAY IN YOUR OVERALL HEALTH

Vitamins are natural substances that are necessary for almost every process in the body. They help trigger thousands of chemical reactions essential to maintaining good health. Because most of these reactions are linked (one triggers another), a missing vitamin or a deficiency of a certain vitamin can cause health problems. Unlike food, vitamins do not provide calories or supply direct energy, but they do assist the calories in carbohydrates, proteins, and fats to produce energy.

Vitamins are found in a wide variety of foods, with some foods being better sources than others. Ideally, you should acquire all the vitamins your body requires through a healthy, balanced diet, as discussed in Chapters 9 and 10. However, if you're like most people, you may fall short in certain areas, in which case you may benefit from vitamin supplements.

WHY YOU MAY NEED VITAMIN SUPPLEMENTS

Some people are more likely to need vitamins than others. Here's a list of people who may want to consider a multivitamin and mineral supplement:

- Strict vegetarians may need extra calcium, iron, zinc, vitamin B_{12}, and vitamin D.
- Women with heavy menstrual bleeding may need additional iron.
- Menopausal women may need calcium supplements.
- People on a low-calorie diet may require supplements.
- People over sixty may experience decreased absorption of numerous vitamins and minerals.
- People who suffer from lactose intolerance or milk allergies may need vitamin D and a calcium supplement.
- People who regularly smoke and/or drink alcohol may not be absorbing certain vitamins and minerals.
- Pregnant or nursing mothers often need additional vitamins and minerals.
- People with impaired nutrient absorption, such as those with celiac disease, may need supplements. Anyone in those categories should definitely consult his or her doctor.

In general, taking a 100 percent vitamin and mineral supplement is the best route to go. This way, you are offering your body the full spectrum of vitamins and minerals, which should cover any basic needs that may not be fulfilled as part of your daily diet. While you are relatively safe taking a multivitamin and mineral supplements, when you want to boost your intake of specific vitamins take time to ask your doctor if there are any possible side effects or dangerous levels that you should avoid. Also, if you take medication, it is particularly important to make sure elevated levels of vitamins will not adversely affect the medication. Some vitamins can be toxic when taken in huge doses, so make sure you review it with your doctor or at least carefully read the labels on the bottles.

Gobble, Gobble

We all love Thanksgiving for the release of serotonin that comes from eating turkey loaded with tryptophan, but have you ever met its cousin, 5-hydroxytryptophan (5-HTP)? You probably didn't know that your body uses the tryptophan you eat to quickly produce 5-HTP in your brain, or that this marvelous chemical is also available in supplements. Extra tryptophan in your diet leads to extra serotonin in your brain, which is why the supplements are touted as a sleep aid and mood lifter, among other things. Foods that provide tryptophan include roasted white turkey, ground beef, cottage cheese, chicken thighs, eggnog, milk, and almonds.

WHY YOUR BRAIN NEEDS VITAMINS AND MINERALS

Your brain needs just as many vitamins and minerals as the rest of your body does, and it relies on your bloodstream to provide them. When vitamin or mineral absorption is insufficient, reduced, or impeded as a result of a poor diet or an illness, your brain is one of the first organs to feel it. Here's a short list of essential vitamins and minerals needed for long-term brain health, and a list of foods that offer the best sources. Again, if you choose to supplement your diet with vitamins or minerals in pill or liquid form, consult with your doctor for safe dosage amounts and to determine if adding them will adversely effect your current medication.

Vitamin A

This antioxidant helps protect brain cells from harmful free radicals and benefits the circulatory system so blood flow to the brain remains strong. There are two forms of vitamin A:

1. **Retinol** is called preformed vitamin A because it is found in animal foods and is readily available to the body. Foods rich in vitamin A (retinol) include beef liver, eggs, milk fortified with vitamin A, other vitamin A–fortified foods, fish oil, margarine, and cheese.

2. **Carotenoids** are another form of vitamin A, which includes beta-carotene. Beta-carotene is the carotenoid most readily converted by the body to vitamin A. Beta-carotene is found in plant foods that are orange, red, dark yellow, and some that are dark green. Foods rich in vitamin A (beta-carotene) include sweet potatoes, carrots, kale, spinach, apricots, cantaloupe, broccoli, and winter squash.

A Gathering of Bs

Vitamin B could very well stand for "vitamin brain." B vitamins (1, 2, 3, 6, and 12) all offer individual support to your brain, but when taken in conjunction with one another, you can boost their individual benefits to the highest level. Bs are vital because they help maintain healthy brain cells, metabolize the carbohydrates used as fuel to the brain, produce neurotransmitters, and improve your moods. People lacking in essential B vitamins have shown an increased risk for depression, anxiety, memory loss, irritability, confusion, abnormal brain waves, and Alzheimer's disease.

Too much preformed vitamin A can be toxic, so consult with your doctor on your desirable dosage.

Vitamin B_{12} (Cobalamin)

An estimated 25 percent of people between ages sixty and seventy are deficient in this essential nutrient, as are nearly 40 percent of people eighty and older. A B_{12} deficiency may be mistaken for an age-related decline in mental function, including confusion, memory loss, and a reduction in reasoning skills. Low levels can also lead to depression, and even psychosis. If you're over fifty, it's worth checking with your doctor to see if you could benefit from taking additional B vitamin supplements.

B Happy

According to findings by the Women's Health and Aging Study, older women with vitamin B_{12} deficiency appear to be more prone to depression. Experts studied 700 women sixty-five and older, and those with a B_{12} deficiency were more than twice as likely to suffer from severe depression than women without a deficiency. Evidently, a lack of B_{12} may cause a buildup of serotonin in neurons that has trouble being released normally. If you're experiencing the blues on a regular basis, ask your doctor to check your vitamin B_{12} levels.

If a supplement is not right for you, look for foods containing a high amount of folic acid, which can serve as a substitute for B_{12}. Foods rich in B_{12} include eggs, milk, clams, liver, beef, oysters, sole, crab, and tuna. As such, vegetarians may need supplemental vitamins.

Vitamin B_6

This important vitamin helps convert sugar into glucose, which the brain needs for fuel. It enables your body to resist stress, helps maintain the proper chemical balance in the body's fluids, works with other vitamins and minerals to supply the energy used by muscles, and is influential in cell growth. It has also been shown to improve general circulation, which can improve memory. Those deficient in B$_6$ could experience headaches, irritability, confusion, and depression.

Foods high in vitamin B$_6$ include wheat germ, cantaloupe, avocados, bananas, carrots, fish, lentils, liver, beef, rice, soybeans, and whole grains.

Vitamin B$_1$ (Thiamine)

Thiamine is needed to help produce energy from the carbohydrates that you eat. Like B$_{12}$, this nutrient is a potent antioxidant. It also is required for numerous metabolic processes within the brain and peripheral nervous system, as well as normal functioning of all body cells, especially nerves. Deficiency is rare, but if you fall short on your needs, it could result in fatigue, emotional instability, loss of energy, nerve damage, muscle weakness, and impaired growth.

Riboflavin to the Rescue

Taking 400 milligrams of riboflavin (also known as vitamin B$_2$) every day may help prevent migraine headaches. In one study, people who took riboflavin supplements for three months had 37 percent fewer migraines than those taking a placebo. Researchers caution, however, that it is only indicated for people whose headaches are true migraines and those who suffer at least twice a month. For those with diagnosed migraines, you might want to ask your doctor if you could try riboflavin supplements.

Foods rich in thiamine (vitamin B$_1$) include whole-grain foods, oatmeal, enriched-grain foods, fortified cereals, brewer's yeast, wheat germ, beef liver, pork, peanuts, and sunflower seeds.

Folic Acid

This nutrient, also a member of the B vitamin family, is known to aid circulation of the blood in the brain by inhibiting narrowing of the arteries in the neck. Studies also suggest that daily supplements of folic acid can reduce the likelihood of certain age-related problems, including dementia. However, normally eating foods high in folic acid can mask a B_{12} deficiency caused by disease, so be sure that your B_{12} levels are tested before beginning a folic acid regime.

Vitamin C

Vitamin C is loaded with goodies. For one, it may prevent the oxidation of LDL (the "bad" cholesterol), which can clog arteries and lead to a heart attack or stroke. Vitamin C may also prevent blood vessels from constricting and thus cutting off blood supply to your heart—and your brain. In one study of individuals with diseased arteries, taking 500 milligrams of supplemental vitamin C per day for a month completely normalized the blood flow in their arteries.

This well-known antioxidant (which basically conducts scavenger missions for free radicals it can gobble up and dissipate) is also extremely important for proper brain function and, as such, is found in much higher levels within the brain than other parts of the body. In addition to boosting the effectiveness of other antioxidants, vitamin C is an essential ingredient in the manufacture of several neurotransmitters such as dopamine and acetylcholine. In short, a daily dose of vitamin C can boost and maintain mental acuity. So important is vitamin C to proper brain function that it is being evaluated as a possible nutritional preventative for Alzheimer's disease.

Foods high in vitamin C include hot chili peppers (raw), cantaloupe, sweet peppers, kiwi, oranges, and mango.

Vitamin D

We've all heard of seasonal affective disorder (SAD), as it has become common knowledge that decreased exposure to sunlight, such as what occurs in winter, can diminish people's sense of well-being—and even lead to a serious depression. SAD can be largely alleviated when your exposure to sunlight is increased (there are also lights you can buy that simulate sunlight) or when you take a vitamin D supplement. Lots of people may be suffering from SAD without realizing that it may be due to their bodies' inability to manufacture the amount of vitamin D they need.

An insufficient supply of vitamin D can have significant effects on how your brain functions. In a study of 1,000 participants (aged sixty-five to ninety-nine) conducted at Tufts University, the 35 percent who had sufficient vitamin D had higher cognitive performance on brain function tests, even after considering other variables that could also affect cognitive performance. Researchers found metabolic pathways for vitamin D in the hippocampus and cerebellum, two areas essential to planning, processing, and forming new memories. Vitamin D also seems to have anti-inflammatory effects that may help keep blood vessels healthy, ensuring nutrient- and oxygen-rich blood flow to brain cells.

Being exposed to sunlight for fifteen minutes a day often provides your body what it needs to manufacture sufficient vitamin D, but those living in areas where sunlight is limited or whose exposure is limited for other reasons may need supplements. Foods high in vitamin D include cod liver oil, oysters, mackerel, and other fish.

Warning: Because vitamin D is a fat-soluble vitamin, larger supplemented doses can damage your kidneys and cause kidney stones. Excess D can also weaken your muscles and bones, and cause excessive bleeding or other health problems. If you take a supplement that includes vitamin D, make sure it does not contain more than 2,000 IU per day. Better yet, check with your doctor before adding D supplements.

Vitamin E

Vitamin E is a natural antioxidant substance that also devours free radicals. It also restores damaged neurotransmitter receptor sites on neurons, which means that vitamin E both prevents age-related brain deterioration and also reverses a specific aspect of that breakdown. There is also evidence that while vitamin E has not been proven to prevent Alzheimer's disease or Parkinson's disease, it can slow its progression once it develops. A combination of vitamin E and the mineral selenium have been shown to dramatically improve mood and cognitive function in older patients. In addition, vitamin E can help reduce risk of heart disease, stroke, and certain types of cancer.

Pick Up the Flax

If you need to sharpen your focus, try taking one tablespoon of ground flaxseed daily. It's an excellent source of alpha-linolenic acid (ALA), a healthy fat that improves the workings of the cerebral cortex, the area of the brain that processes sensory information, including that of pleasure. To meet your daily quota, sprinkle it on salads or mix it into a smoothie or shake.

Luckily, vitamin E is found in many foods and is most abundant in dried almonds, hazelnuts, walnuts, wheat germ oil, sunflower oil, fish liver oils, peanut butter, whole grains, sweet potatoes, and green leafy vegetables.

Calcium

Calcium is one of the minerals that plays a significant role in your brain's ability to function at peak capacity. Basically, it facilitates the production of nerve tissue, helps regulate your heartbeat and your metabolic rate, and is absolutely vital for the proper transmission of messages between your neurons. Calcium plays a role in releasing neurotransmitters and improving synaptic connections. Calcium is found in dairy products, kidney beans, salmon, bok choy, broccoli, and almonds.

Magnesium

Proper brain function depends on a constant supply of biochemical energy, which is created by exchanged charged particles, known as ions, across the cell membrane of nerves. The most critical ions in this process are sodium, potassium, calcium, and magnesium. While sodium, potassium, and calcium are present in a lot of the foods we eat, finding a good supply of magnesium is often difficult.

To begin with, a big part of American diets (fats, meats, and dairy products) are low in magnesium. Processing or cooking further reduces its levels in food, and not all of the magnesium we do consume is absorbed.

However, your brain needs magnesium to build the sheaths that insulate the nerve fibers. It is also essential to the electrical activity of nerve cells, as well as to the very existence of a cell: without the proper balance of magnesium, neurons can become overstimulated and burst. There are more than 300 different enzymes in the human body that require magnesium to function, and a great many are found in your brain. Magnesium aids in the conduction of nerve impulses, the transmission of the neurotransmitter glutamate, and achieving neuroplasticity. It also regulates a key receptor in the hippocampus that aids memory and learning.

Magnesium is also a powerhouse mineral when it comes to maintaining metabolism, converting sugar into energy, and helping your body absorb calcium, vitamin C, phosphorous, sodium, and potassium.

The most optimum levels of magnesium can be found in wheat and oat bran, brown rice, Florida avocados, almonds, cashews, and other nuts, pumpkin seeds, and fresh, leafy spinach.

Selenium and Zinc

Two other minerals that are helpful to your brain are selenium and zinc. Selenium serves as a powerful antioxidant by preventing the oxidation of fat, which helps slow down age-related brain deterioration and preserve cognitive functions. It may also help with circulation throughout your body and bolster your immune system, and it has been studied intensely as a cancer-preventative mineral. The best sources of selenium are Brazil nuts and walnuts. Tuna, oily fish, and shellfish are otherwise good sources. However, be careful: Eating too much selenium results in a toxic disorder known as selenosis.

Zinc helps your brain by assisting in the elimination of free radicals, strengthening neuronal membranes, and cleansing your brain of residue from environmental lead exposure. Good sources of zinc include oysters, beef, pumpkin (especially seeds), yogurt, wheat, and nuts.

SUPPLEMENTS THAT BENEFIT YOUR BRAIN

In recent years, neuroscientists and nutritionists have conducted studies to determine the effects of various supplements on the brain. We're not discussing all of them, only a few that relate specifically to happiness, or at least mood alteration. Again, in some cases, we're offering suggested dosages for these supplements, but ask your doctor before adding anything. Your doctor should be the person who gives you recommendations for an effective yet safe dosage. This particularly applies to anyone taking heart-related, anxiety, or antidepressant medications.

GABA

GABA, short for gamma-aminobutyric acid, is an amino acid that also functions as a neurotransmitter, acting primarily as an inhibitor during highly stressful times. It helps stabilize nerve cells by decreasing their ability to fire erratically or excessively and by increasing calming alpha waves and decreasing beta waves. Low GABA levels or decreased GABA activity in the brain has been associated with anxiety, depression, and insomnia. Relaxation methods, such as meditation or yoga, may enhance the benefits of GABA. Dosages can range from 250 milligrams to 1,500 milligrams a day, divided into three doses for ideal absorption. Check with your doctor first.

SAMe

If your brain is functioning well, it produces all the SAMe (short for S-adenosylmethionine) it needs to assist with the production of brain compounds, including neurotransmitters. Often, however, those suffering from depression seem to have a problem producing enough SAMe. Taking SAMe supplements seems to improve your brain's ability to produce the neurotransmitters required to stave off depression, as well as improve cell membrane fluidity. Some studies have found it to be as effective as antidepressant medications in treating depression and fibromyalgia, a chronic muscle pain disorder that is often treated with low-dosage antidepressants. Recommended dosage is 200–400 milligrams two to four times a day. Check with your doctor first.

How about Those Amino Acids?

Your brain health also relies on certain amino acids, organic compounds that help make proteins and are essential to your metabolism. Some amino acids play a vital role in how your brain functions, often affecting neurotransmitters and memory. While we don't recommend rushing out to buy supplements, you may want to discuss them with your doctor if you notice any weaknesses related to the amino acids noted below:

- **Arginine.** This amino acid is partially converted into a chemical known as spermine, which helps your brain process memory. Low levels of spermine often signal age-related memory loss.
- **Choline.** The brain uses this amino acid to manufacture acetylcholine, a memory-related neurotransmitter. As you age, your body produces less acetylcholine, so you may want to consider a supplement. Dietary sources of choline include cabbage, cauliflower, eggs, peanuts, and lecithin.
- **Glutamine.** This amino acid is a precursor to GABA, one of your calming neurotransmitters. It also helps improve clarity of thought and boosts alertness by assisting in the manufacture of glutamic acid, a compound known for its ability to eliminate metabolic wastes in the brain.
- **Methionine.** Like glutamine, this amino acid helps cleanse your brain of damaging metabolic wastes. It is an effective antioxidant and helps reduce brain levels of dangerous heavy metals such as mercury.

Inositol

Inositol is a natural brain biochemical that appears to help neurons maximize use of serotonin. In various studies, inositol supplements have been shown to improve depression, generalized anxiety, panic disorder, and obsessive-compulsive disorder.

St. John's Wort

St. John's wort is an herb that has shown some effectiveness in increasing serotonin availability in your brain, which helps to lift moods and perhaps even moderate the symptoms of depression by decreasing the amount of cingulate gyrus hyperactivity.

Have a Cuppa . . . Herbal Tea

Herbal teas have been brewed for thousands of years because thousands have found that they can boost your mood in subtle and not-so-subtle ways. Here are a few varieties to consider:

- Catnip tea—relaxant and mild depressant
- Cinnamon tea—clears the brain and improves thought processes
- Ginseng tea—natural tonic for a lift
- Jasmine tea—mild nerve sedative
- Sage tea—improves brain nourishment, known as the thinker's tea

Ginkgo Biloba

Ginkgo biloba has been used in China for thousands of years to improve brain functioning, and maybe they've been onto something big. In a study published in the *Journal of the American Medical Association*, researchers confirmed that people who take the ginkgo extract for mild to severe dementia may improve both their ability to remember and to interact socially. Gingko biloba has also been used to enhance blood circulation and improve muscle tone in the walls of blood vessels. Furthermore, ginkgo biloba may increase sexual appetite and performance, and that can certainly lead to increased happiness! However, adverse effects have been shown for those taking antidepressants and heart medications, so check with your doctor before taking ginkgo biloba supplements.

The Anxiety Cocktail

Before you begin taking antianxiety medication, you might want to consider taking meditation classes, which can help you learn relaxation techniques, along with taking natural supplements. Gamma-aminobutyric acid (GABA), vitamin B_6, glutamine, valerian, or kava could prove helpful in alleviating your symptoms. Fish oil supplements, particularly 2,000–4,000 milligrams of EPA, and extra vitamin D may also prove beneficial. Ask your doctor for specific dosage suggestions.

The Depression Cocktail

Before you take antidepressants, do your brain a favor and add daily exercise to your daily rituals. Exercise boosts blood flow to your brain and often improves your mood (the more aerobic the better). As with anxiety, omega-3 fish oil supplements and vitamin D will likely assist, as will supplements that boost serotonin, such as 5-hydroxytryptophan (5-HTP), L-tryptophan, and inositol. Add exercise first, and if it doesn't quite do the trick, ask your doctor for approved supplements and dosages.

SPICE IT UP!

There are, of course, hundreds of macro- and micronutrients that could directly and indirectly affect your brain health. We've covered the ones that we felt were most relevant to training your brain to be happy, but new information is always being accumulated, particularly as more attention is being paid to your brain's ability to grow.

We always recommend talking with your doctor about any and all concerns, but also to be informed about the latest science. We don't recommend fads or trying any supplements without fully researching side effects and determining how anything you add will affect whatever medications you are already taking.

In general, if you eat a healthy diet, add a lot of superfoods, and supplement only where necessary, you and your brain should be both healthy and happy. Whatever you do, remember that your brain may not be visible to your naked eye, but it plays a vital role in every aspect of your life. Nurture it well, and it will definitely reward you.

CONCLUSION

USE WHAT YOU'VE LEARNED TO GET HAPPY!

We are nearing the end of our happiness journey together. Before we sign off, we wanted to offer you a brief summary that you can use to easily refresh your memory.

MEET YOUR BRAIN

Your brain is the highest achievement of evolution, and it's what makes you human. You are born with a brain that has the ability to learn pretty much anything. It is like the world's best multitool, with the ability to process your environment, make rules, keep you healthy, and, most importantly, keep you happy.

The most important brain centers for your happiness are your limbic brain—areas like the hypothalamus, nucleus accumbens, hippocampus, and the amygdala—and your neocortex, especially your left PFC, which sits as the CEO, telling other brain areas what to do.

CELEBRATE YOUR BRAIN!

Your brain has the ability to change and adapt throughout your entire life, and *you* have the ability to use your mind in order to direct the course of this neuroplastic change. Your brain is capable of growing new neurons through the process of neurogenesis, reprogramming old connections and changing the strength of your desires, learning, growing, and changing throughout your entire life and into your golden years, and *willing* your way into a better and more satisfying life.

TECHNIQUES YOU CAN USE TO TRAIN YOUR BRAIN

We've discussed many techniques that utilize this great mind/brain connection to help you start on the journey to a happier you. These include:

- Cognitive behavioral therapy
- Meditation, particularly mindfulness meditation
- Techniques to improve your sleeping habits

- Ideas to improve your thought processing
- Ways to recognize and control your emotions
- Suggestions for play and recreational activities
- Tips for providing the best nutrition for your brain

BREAKTHROUGHS IN NEUROSCIENCE

As a final reminder, here are the most important breakthroughs in neuroscience that help us understand why these techniques work. Here's how you can utilize each amazing aspect of your incredible brain:

Neurogenesis

What it is: The ability to create new neurons throughout your life.

How to use it in everyday life: By maximizing opportunities to explore new avenues in learning, you can help your brain create neurons specific to each new task. Or, you can hone your mind in on whatever work or interest you are currently pursuing, as focusing intently and often will strengthen existing neuronal synapses and create new ones.

Neuroplasticity

What it is: The ability to strengthen, weaken, and change neural connections throughout your life.

How to use it in everyday life: You don't need to make new neurons in order to change your brain (although it certainly helps!). You can rewire the connections that are already present, making them stronger or weaker depending upon your actions and the focus on your thoughts. Neurons that fire together, wire together—and those that are no longer used become weak. Thus, your brain can adapt to whatever comes in life, and you can focus and strengthen the parts of your brain that matter most to you.

Mind Over Gray Matter

What it is: Your brain can reshape itself and form new synapses purely from thinking thoughts.

How to use it in everyday life: Although it was long believed that only external influences could change the brain, now we know that this is not true. Your ability to create, visualize, and empathize is just as powerful a brain changer as the influences of the outside world. The way that you think—whether with happy or sad patterns—trains your brain into thinking that way more easily and robustly as time passes and habits form. Changing your thinking patterns changes your brain structure, and you can shape your brain to better serve you in the new, happy life that you design.

Imagination Is Reality

What it is: Your brain cannot differentiate between situations that you are merely thinking about and things that are actually occurring.

How to use it in everyday life: If you spend the time to think and focus upon what you want to happen—the way you'd like a conversation to go, or the way you want to act at a party, or doing well at a new hobby—your brain will fire as if you were actually doing what you think about, strengthening synapses between brain areas as well as your muscles and organs. This makes it easier for you to actually perform any action that you desire, because your brain and body are already primed and raring to go! You can imagine yourself into a happier state of mind.

Mindfulness Meditation

What it is: Focusing on thoughts as butterflies and concentrating on the here and now helps your mind train your brain to feel happier.

How to use it in everyday life: Making time for mindfulness meditation will allow you to calm the limbic centers of your brain that are in charge of fear and anxiety, such as the amygdala, and strengthen connections to the PFC, allowing you better mental control over your emotions and granting you the ability to live in the moment, free from stress and unwanted emotions.

Cognitive Behavioral Therapy (CBT)

What it is: The ability to work with thoughts and behaviors to change the way you cope psychologically.

How to use it in everyday life: By using the belief that *your reactions* to thoughts are what cause emotions, you can train yourself to focus on the cognitive content of your reaction to upsetting events or streams of thought. Concentrating on your reactions to internal or external events will allow you better control over your negative emotions and allow you to truly tune in to the life events and thoughts that make you happy.

HAPPY TRAILS!

So there you have it! We're very confident that *you* can successfully train your brain to get happier, and we wish you all good luck along the way!

Go on now, get happy!

INDEX

A

Acetylcholine, 36
Alkon, Daniel, 51
Alpha brain waves, 38
Altman, Joseph, 18
Alzheimer's disease, 29
Amen, Daniel, 73, 122
Amygdala, 33, 55, 113
Anatomy of an Illness (Cousins), 145
Antidepressants, 5
Antioxidants, 175, 188, 189, 208, 214, 223
Antipsychotic drugs, 5
Anxiety, 55
Aristotle, 3–4, 9–10, 90
The Art of Happiness (Dalai Lama), 89
Aurelius, Marcus, 9
Authentic Happiness (Seilgman), 48
Autonomic nervous system (involuntary), 54–55
Avicenna (Islamic philosopher), 10

B

Baby boomers, 8
Baraz, James, 148
Basal ganglia, 34–35
Bayer, Shirley, 18
Beck, Aaron T., 62, 72
Behaviors, 59–61
Beta brain waves, 37
Brain, the, 23–41
    aberrant chemistry of, 6

activity monitoring and, 16–17
alcohol and, 198–99
anatomy of, 24–26, 46
anterior cingulate cortex and, 32–33
atrophy and, 69
basal ganglia and, 34–35
cerebellum, 31
complex functions and, 23
deep limbic system of, 33–34
deep structures of, 31–35
defined, 43–44
drugs and, 199–200
eating and, 173, 175
emotional information and, 32–33
gratitude and, 123
health of, 32–33
hippocampus and, 29
integration center of, 28
limbic system of, 25
lobes of, 26–31
meditation and, 92–93, 95–96, 102–04
motor control and, 34–35
negative thought patterns and, 68–70
neocortex system of, 25–26
nutrition and, 184–85
playing and, 136
preprogramed/preorganized, 10–11
reptilian system of, 25
reshaping thoughts of, 15
science of, 1, 11–13

stimulating activities and, 137–38, 140–41

stress and, 139

Happiness, sleeping for, 151–71

brain and, 157–58

brain plasticity and, 158, 162

dreaming and, 164–65

hazards of too little sleep and, 156

importance of sleep and, 153–54

learning/memory and, 163

memory and, 162

new moms and, 159

quantity/quality and, 160

reasons for sleep and, 154–55

REM sleep and, 163

sleep deprivation and, 158

sleep drugs and, 167

sleep problems and, 168–69

sleep quantity and, 158–60

sleep triggers and, 168

stages of sleep and, 160–62

stress and, 169

what not to do and, 165–66

what to do and, 166–68

Happiness, superfoods for, 205–15

antioxidants and, 208

apples as, 209

blueberries as, 208

brain performance and, 205

chocolate as, 212–14

depression and, 207

eggs as, 210–11

fish as, 206–08

nuts as, 209–10

oats as, 212

omega-3 and, 206, 207, 208

quinoa as, 210–11

soy as, 212

Happiness, thinking for, 65–87

mindfulness and, 83–86

negative thought patterns and, 68–70

optimism and, 70–71

positive, 70–71

thoughts/feelings and, 67–68

turning negative to positive and, 69–70

.See also Cognitive behavioral therapy (CBT)

Happiness, vitamins/minerals for, 217–31

brain health and, 219–26

role of, 217–18

supplements and, 218–19, 227–30

Happiness Now (Holden), 118

Happy brain quiz, 1–3

Happy eat quiz, 173–75

Happy sleep quiz, 151–53

Hebb, Donald, 19

Hebb's law, 19

Hill, Napoleon, 71

Hippocampus, 29, 70

Hippocrates, 1, 3

Holden, Robert, 118

Hypothalamus, 33

I

Imagination, 20–21, 236

Integrative Medicine (Rakel), 131

J

Johnstone, Brick, 104

K

Kabat-Zinn, Jon, 84, 95–96
Kaplan, Michael, 18

L

Locke, John, 10
Love and Will (May), 91
Lykken, David T., 113

M

Magnetic resonance imagery (MRI), 5
Maji, Husseini, 69
May, Rollo, 91
Mayberg, Helen, 70, 71
Memories
    connections and, 51
    explicit, 50
    false, 53
    formation of, 49–53
    happy, 162
    implicit, 49
    location of, 50–51
    new, 69, 70, 224
    reactivating, 52–53
    short-term/long-term, 29
    thoughts and, 63
Mendius, Dr., 119
Merzenich, Mike, 70
Millionaires vs. slum dwellers, 7
Mind, defined, 44
Mindfulness-based cognitive therapy, 83–86
Mindfulness meditation, 16, 84–85, 95–101, 104–05, 236
Mind science, 9–11

N

Modernization, 6
Molaison, Henry G., 52
Moods, 57
Moreau, Jeanne, 217
Mulholland, Thomas, 39
Myers, David, 122

Negative thought patterns, 68–70
Neocortex, 31–32
Nervous systems, 53–54
Neurogenesis, 17–19, 235
Neuromodulators, 36
Neuronal activity/compassion, 16–17
Neurons, 19–20, 24, 36
Neuroplasticity, 11–14, 61, 90, 95, 226, 235
    See also Plasticity
Neuroscience, ix–x, 15, 16, 43, 235–37
Neuroscience/psychobiology, 8–9
Neurotransmitters, 36, 116
Newberg, Andrew, 92
Nottebohm, Fernando, 18
Nutrition
    brain and, 184–85
    deficiency and, 175
    fruits/vegetables and, 187–88
    knowledge of, 176
    super foods and, 205
    USDA Food Pyramid and, 178
    See also Food choices; Happiness, eating for; Happiness, super-foods for

ON TOP

Getting Where Women Really Belong

- Trying to lose the losers you've been dating?
- Striving to find the time to be a doting mother, dedicated employee, and still be a hot piece of you-know-what in the bedroom?
- Been in a comfortable relationship that's becoming, well, too comfortable?

Don't despair! Visit the Jane on Top blog—your new source for information (and commiseration) on all things relationships, sex, and the juggling act that is being a modern gal.

Sign up for our newsletter at
www.adamsmedia.com/blog/relationships
and download a **Month-ful of Happiness!**
That's 30 days of free tips guaranteed to lift your mood!